VIKTOR FRANKL

VIKTOR FRANKL

A LIFE WORTH LIVING

by ANNA REDSAND

Clarion Books
New York

PICTURE CREDITS

Claus Dettelbacher: p. 57

Fotoarchiv Media Wien: pp. 5, 35, 87

Freud Museum, London: p. 19

IMAGNO/Austrian Archives: p. 107

IMAGNO/Franz Hubmann: p. 100

IMAGNO/Viktor Frankl Archive: pp. iii, 8, 11, 12, 20, 33, 53, 59, 79, 84, 89, 102, 105, 108
115, 116, 118, 128, 134 (photographer: Katharina Vesely)

János Kalmár: pp. 111, 120, 124, 131

Library of Congress: p. 27

United States Holocaust Memorial Museum, courtesy of the following:
Archiwum Dokumentacji Mechanicznej: p. 62;
Ivan Vojtech Fric: pp. 65, 93;
Ralph Harpuder: pp. 91, 104; KZ Gedenkstaette Dachau (photographer: Fritz Melbach): p. 3; Frank Manucci: p. 2;
General Anthony McAullife Estate: p. 80; William O. McWorkman: p. 14; Jack Moses: p. 73; National Archives and
Records Administration, College Park (NARA): pp. 39, 41, 45, 48, 69, 71, 74, 81; Miriam Patipa: p. 66;
Robert A. Schmuhl: p. 95; Bud Tullin: p. 22; Dr. Adolf Vees: p. 46; Henry Wellisch: p. 32

Viktor Frankl Estate: p. 30

.

Clarion Books
a Houghton Mifflin Company imprint
215 Park Avenue South, New York, NY 10003
Copyright © 2006 by Anna Redsand

The text was set in 14-point Fournier Monotype.
Book design by Trish Parcell Watts.
Maps on pages 51 and 57 by Trish Parcell Watts.

For information about permission to reproduce selections from this book,
write to Permissions, Houghton Mifflin Company, 215 Park Avenue South, New York, NY 10003.

www.clarionbooks.com

Printed in the U.S.A.

Library of Congress Cataloging-in-Publication Data
Redsand, Anna.
Viktor Frankl : a life worth living / Anna Redsand.
p. cm.
Includes bibliographical references and index.
ISBN-13: 978-0-618-72343-0   ISBN-10: 0-618-72343-9
1. Frankl, Viktor Emil. 2. Psychotherapists—Austria—Biography.
3. Holocaust survivors—Austria—Biography. I. Title.
RC438.6.F73R43 2006
616.89' 140092—dc22
2006006273

VB 10 9 8 7 6 5 4 3 2 1

Title page: Viktor Frankl, around 1960, lecturing.

To my daughter,

Cheyenne Jansdatter,

and

to the students of

Cesar Chavez Community School,

who give so much meaning to my life

CONTENTS

ACKNOWLEDGMENTS

I am grateful to everyone who has been part of the creation of this book. Viktor Frankl provided all the inspiration. Elly Frankl opened her home and invited Harald Mori along. Jean Hedberg, Cheyenne Jansdatter, Linden McNeilly, and Suzanne Norman read early versions of the manuscript and gave valuable feedback. Jennifer Greene, my editor, shares the vision of every American high school student reading *Man's Search for Meaning*. She asked the questions that made this a better book. Joann Hill knows how to make a book beautiful. Eleni Beja made things move smoothly. Rita Apsan, János Kalmár, Gerald Piffl, Maren L. Read, Franz Vesely, Michael Wenusch, and especially my colleague Anne Egger, patiently helped provide the photos and other illustrations and got them into usable format. Irene Dauphinee made the trip to Vienna possible, and I am grateful to her for always believing in me.

INTRODUCTION

SALVATION THROUGH LOVE

The icy wind whistled at the prisoners' backs, pushing through the threadbare rags their captors called clothing. They shivered as they marched, stumbling over stones, sloshing through freezing puddles. The guards shouted, "Left-two-three-four, left-two-three-four," and drove the men with rifle butts when they slowed or slipped in the mud.

Occasionally, prisoner number 119,104 dared to glance at the stars fading into the pink edges of the horizon. Suddenly, the man next to him whispered, "If our wives could see us now! I do hope they are better off in their camps and don't know what is happening to us."

When he heard these words, Viktor Frankl, prisoner number

119,104, no longer saw the fading stars or felt the icy water bite his ankles. Instead, he saw the sparkling dark eyes and curly black hair of his wife, Tilly, who reminded him of a Spanish dancer. He saw Tilly smile, saw her look at him with encouragement. Her caring look shone more brightly for him than the sun that was beginning to light the sky.

Viktor thought then of the thousands of songs and poems that say love represents the best in people. When he least expected it, on the muddy path from the concentration camp barracks to the ditch he and the other prisoners would be digging that day, Viktor Frankl felt that for the first time in his life he fully understood the immense power of love.

The day wore on, and it seemed to be the same as every other day in the camp: prisoners fell and were beaten by the guards; the men, with little food in their stomachs, hacked at the frozen ground with worn-out tools; they heard the guards shout at them, calling them pigs. Inside Viktor, though, something had changed. He spent the

Emaciated survivors of Dachau Concentration Camp immediately after the war.

day dreaming that he was talking with Tilly. He asked her questions, and she responded. She questioned him, and he answered.

At one point, it occurred to Viktor that he didn't even know if Tilly was still alive. The last time he had seen her was at the Auschwitz concentration camp in Poland. He remembered how gracefully she had calmed the other prisoners on the way from the Theresienstadt camp to Auschwitz. He remembered how defiantly she had smashed her gold watch and how, together, they had thrown away their gold wedding bands to keep the Nazis from getting them. Viktor realized, as he struggled to break the icy ground with his shovel, that he didn't need to know whether Tilly was alive. He knew that love does not require the physical presence of the person who is loved. In that moment, love was his salvation.

Viktor's realization that, for him, love was what made life worth living took place sometime between October 1944 and March 1945 in Kaufering Camp. The end of World War II was approaching. Under the Nazi rule of Adolf Hitler, Germany had conquered,

Concentration-camp prisoners on a forced march at the very end of the war. Judging from their appearance of relative health, it is possible that they had only recently been sent to the camps.

occupied, and, by this time, nearly lost most of the countries of Europe. During the twelve years that Hitler was dictator, from 1933 to 1945, he put into effect the most systematic killing of innocent people ever known to humankind. People who spoke out against Nazi policies, Jews, homosexuals, Eastern Europeans, and Roma (commonly known as Gypsies) were put in concentration camps throughout Europe. There, they were used for slave labor, starved, tortured, shot, and gassed to death. Eleven million people, six million of them Jews, lost their lives in this death machine, known today as the Holocaust. People like Viktor Frankl, who survived, found that their lives had been forever changed.

Viktor Frankl had been trained as a physician, specializing in psychiatry and neurology, before he and his family were deported to Nazi concentration camps. As a young medical student, Viktor had organized suicide-prevention centers for teenagers in his home city of Vienna, Austria. Later, over the course of four years, he was in charge of the treatment of approximately twelve thousand depressed women, many of whom were suicidal.

Viktor's work with suicidal people and people with other emotional problems led him to develop a new kind of treatment, which he named *logotherapy*. A basic principle of logotherapy is that finding meaning in life can enable a person to survive even the worst conditions. As a psychiatrist, Viktor believed that his task was to help the suicidal teens and women in his care find meaning in their lives. But the greatest test of his theories came during his own horror-filled experiences in four concentration camps. He used the principles of logotherapy over and over again to help himself and his fellow prisoners survive their ordeal.

A few months after his release from the last camp, Türkheim, on April 27, 1945, Viktor wrote a book about his time as a prisoner of the Nazis. He recorded his psychological analysis of the concentration camp experience and explained how finding something to live for helped prisoners survive. The book, *Man's Search for Meaning*, has been translated from German into twenty-seven languages and has sold more than four million copies in English alone.

Viktor Frankl had had an opportunity to escape the horrors of the concentration camps altogether. Several years before his deportation, he applied for a visa to emigrate to the United States. In 1941, the American embassy called and told him to pick up his visa. By then, many Jews had already been taken to concentration camps. Elderly Jews were being taken first, and Viktor knew his parents might be called up at any time. He had an important job as chief of neurology at the Rothschild Hospital. He knew his position might protect him and his parents from deportation, at least for a while. It was almost certain his mother and father would be taken eventually, and he knew they would need support and care when they were. On the other hand, he felt that if he went to America, he would be able to continue his life's work—developing logotherapy and making it known throughout the world.

Viktor didn't know what to do. Looking for an answer, he walked into St. Stephan's Cathedral in central Vienna. Although he was Jewish, he sought out the church as a quiet place where he could look into his heart. He seated himself in the church's vastness, surrounded by immense granite pillars, brilliant stained-glass windows, and rows of flickering candles. He listened to someone play the huge pipe organ beneath the deep blue and

St. Stephan's Cathedral has been called "the soul of Vienna." It offered Viktor a quiet place to think while he tried to decide whether to leave Austria and escape the Nazis or stay and care for his parents.

red window above the church entrance. All the time, he asked himself, "Should I leave my parents behind? . . . Should I say goodbye and leave them to their fate?" He wondered where his greater responsibility lay—in caring for his parents or in going to America so he could continue his lifework. He left an hour later without an answer, thinking, "Isn't this the kind of situation that requires some hint from heaven?"

When he got home, Viktor found a piece of marble lying on the table. His father told him he had found it in the rubble of one of the synagogues near their home. Nazis and citizens of Vienna had destroyed this and hundreds of other synagogues and Jewish prayer houses. A single Hebrew letter was engraved on the marble. Viktor's father told him that the letter came from one of the Ten Commandments, the only commandment to use that letter. Viktor was eager to hear which one it was, and his father told him: "Honor thy father and thy mother, that thy days may be long upon the land which the Lord thy God giveth thee." Viktor felt that this was the sign he was waiting for. He decided to stay with his parents in Vienna.

If Viktor had escaped the concentration camps by going to America, he would have been spared great suffering. Perhaps logotherapy would have become widely used by psychotherapists. But it is the story of how Viktor Frankl found meaning in the darkest places on earth that has touched the lives of so many people. What he learned and taught the world through his experiences in the concentration camps spread not only to psychotherapists but also to millions of adults and young people throughout the world. Viktor thought he had to choose between caring for his parents and pursuing his life's work. In the end, choosing to care for his parents furthered that work in ways he couldn't have imagined when he made his decision.

ONe

A SCHOLAR AND A PRANKSTER

It was March 26, 1905, a Sunday afternoon, the time of the week when the citizens of Vienna crowded the streets, strolling to their favorite coffeehouses and bakery-cafés. Café Siller at the edge of the Danube Canal was alive with conversation. Groups of people shared their interest in the new literature, art, music, and architecture bursting onto the scene. Gabriel and Elsa Frankl sat at one of the tables, looking up now and then from the books they were reading to exchange ideas over cups of Viennese coffee. In the middle of the conversation, Elsa Frankl felt a strong contraction and told her husband it was time to go home to prepare for the birth of their second child.

The Frankls left their coffee cups and quickly walked home

across the Aspern Bridge and up four flights of stairs. Later that day, Viktor Emil Frankl was born in the family apartment. As an adult, Viktor loved to say, "I was almost born in the famous Café Siller in Vienna."

Both of Viktor's parents were born in what was then Czechoslovakia, which was part of the Austro-Hungarian Empire. Gabriel, whose father was a poor bookbinder, came to Vienna, Austria, to go to high school and medical school, though he was later forced to leave medical school for financial reasons. Instead of becoming a doctor, he went to work as a government employee, eventually becoming the director of the Ministry of Social Service.

Gabriel Frankl had many sides to him: Viktor described his father as a man with strong self-discipline who was nevertheless hot tempered at times. It was common for him to have a positive attitude in the face of difficulties, and at the same time he was a principled perfectionist. Elsa Frankl, Viktor's mother, was kindhearted and deeply pious. She was born Elsa Lion and came from a long line of rabbis, some of whom were famous.

Gabriel and Elsa Frankl were drawn together by their Jewish faith. Although their personalities were very different, they were able to use their faith to create a warm, secure home for their three children. They were not strictly Orthodox Jews, but they always observed Jewish holidays, and they followed Jewish dietary laws until World War I, when the need for food became so great that keeping them was no longer possible. Every morning, Gabriel Frankl went into his room to pray. He put on phylacteries,

Elsa and Gabriel Frankl, in their wedding portrait.

small leather boxes containing verses from the Hebrew Bible. He prayed the Shema Yisrael, the principal prayer of the Jewish faith: "Hear, O Israel, the Lord our God, the Lord is One God; and you shall love the Lord your God with all your heart and with all your soul and with all your strength." Viktor's father's prayers made a deep impression on his son—one that would stay with him for the rest of his life.

The Frankl apartment was on Czerningasse in the mostly Jewish district of Leopoldstadt. It was a narrow street lined on both sides by five-story stucco apartment buildings. Number Six was built around an enclosed courtyard where Viktor played with his older brother, Walter, and his younger sister, Stella. The whole family often took the fifteen-minute walk from home to the Prater amusement park. The part of the park closest to the Frankl home was a collection of sausage stands, beer gardens, game booths, dancing

The Aspern Bridge, shown in a 1927 postcard, crosses the Danube Canal and connects the center of Vienna, where Café Siller was located, with Leopoldstadt, the part of Vienna where the Frankl family lived and where Viktor was born.

This 1928 panorama gives a good view of the double rings of magnificent public buildings of Vienna. The opera house, museums, theaters, and hotels are in the center of the city. The building in the lower left corner is the Upper Belvedere Palace.

cafés, and the world-famous, 212-foot-high *Riesenrad* Ferris wheel. Stretching beyond the amusement section, between the two Danube canals, the park was lined with many beautiful garden paths and filled with tall trees and green lawns where the children could play.

Viktor was as different from his brother and sister as Mr. and Mrs. Frankl were from each other. Walter was two and a half years older than Viktor, and Stella was four years younger. Walter and Stella were tall and sturdily built, while Viktor was small and wiry. Neither Walter nor Stella was very interested in studying; they were more drawn to the arts. As an adult, Walter pursued a career in architecture and interior design, while Stella was interested in women's fashion.

Viktor, on the other hand, had started to tell people by the time he was three that he wanted to be a doctor. Gabriel Frankl was delighted that Viktor might accomplish the dream he had been denied. He and Viktor took long walks around the city, and they often passed the University of Vienna Medical School. When they reached the Anatomical Institute, where medical students were busy dissecting human cadavers, the sharp, sickeningly sweet smell of formaldehyde mixed with dead flesh reached their nostrils. Other people crossed the street to avoid the odor and the gruesome images evoked by the labs. Viktor, however, at age seven or eight, dragged his father toward the lab. He stood by the open windows and breathed in the smells, imagined what was happening inside, and steeled his body to keep from running, exhilarated "by the power of the spirit to overcome the normal reaction."

A 1978 photograph of the apartment building on Czerningasse where the Frankl family lived. Their flat was on the fifth floor.

One day, Viktor and Stella's uncle Erwin gave Stella ten *Heller* (about ten cents). The future doctor thought he saw how he could get that ten-Heller piece for himself. He picked up a red marble and a pair of scissors. Walking up to Stella, he told her he was sure her tonsils were very swollen. The only solution was surgery. He hid the marble in one hand, stuck the scissors into Stella's mouth, and made noises to go with the operation. When he pulled out the scissors, he opened his fist to reveal the red marble—Stella's swollen tonsil. The young surgeon found it convenient to charge his sister ten Heller for the operation.

The Frankl family frequently visited Porolitz, Czechoslovakia, the small town where Viktor's father had been born. Often, Viktor, Walter, and a group of other boys and girls would walk to outlying farms. When they arrived, they quickly began rolling barrels and carrying wooden planks. They upended the barrels and laid the planks across them, carried props onto their makeshift stage, and proceeded to get into costume. On one occasion, they had rehearsed a popular comedy, *Lumpazivagabundus (The Roguish Trio)*, under Walter's direction. Offstage, Viktor donned a bald-headed cap and clambered onto the planks as old Dr. Stieglitz. Then, leaving the stage, he quickly changed costumes and became a drunken cobbler. He portrayed his characters so vividly that one little boy in the audience never forgot how Viktor made him laugh. Many years later, when the little boy had become a psychiatrist, he introduced Viktor at a lecture in Oslo, Norway. The man didn't know much about logotherapy before the lecture, but he remembered the drunken cobbler very well.

While Viktor Frankl was playing with his brother and sister at the Prater, challenging himself on the sidewalk at the Anatomical Institute, occasionally earning a fee as a young "surgeon," and acting in the children's farmyard theater, a young man named Adolf Hitler was living in a hostel for homeless men in Brigittenau.

Viktor, at age five, poses between Walter and Stella.

Brigittenau was the Vienna district next to Leopoldstadt, where the Frankls lived. Hitler had left his family in Linz, an Austrian city west of Vienna. He hoped to fulfill his dream of becoming a painter, but twice he failed the entrance exam to the Academy of Fine Arts. With the loss of his career goal, Hitler was discouraged and desperate. He kept himself alive by shoveling snow in front of the luxurious Imperial Hotel and selling his sketches on the streets.

Austria was then part of the Austro-

Hungarian Empire. The empire's two main ethnic groups were German and Hungarian, but fifteen other ethnicities were also represented. Among them were many Jews and Slavs (people from Eastern European countries like Poland and Czechoslovakia). Many Austrians and Germans wanted to unite Germany, Austria, and the German-speaking parts of other countries under the rule of one government. Hitler passionately believed in this idea, known as the Pan-German Movement. He had grown up in small towns in Austria, where he constantly witnessed anti-Semitism, the hatred and persecution of Jews. He and others combined anti-Semitism with Pan-Germanism. They saw Jews and Slavs as outsiders incapable of becoming true Germans and therefore enemies of German nationalism. As Hitler's poverty and failure deepened, his hatred of Jews grew. He began to believe that the financial success of Jews was responsible for his own poverty. In reality, many Jews were just as poor as Hitler was.

As his life in Vienna spiraled downward, Hitler thought more and more about a long-cherished dream of living in Germany. To him, Germany represented the racial purity he longed for; he found the ethnic diversity of Austria more and more abhorrent. In 1913, with World War I about to begin, Adolf Hitler left Austria and settled in Munich, Germany, without notifying the Austrian military draft. He loved his new life in Germany and was very upset when an Austrian army officer appeared at his door in Munich in January 1914, ordering him to report for duty in his hometown. He appealed the order, but his appeal was denied, and he was required to report for a physical examination. When he showed up, the recruiters decided he looked physically run-down and weak, and on that basis he was declared unfit for military service.

Nearly seven months later, a member of a Serbian terrorist group assassinated Archduke Francis Ferdinand, the heir to the Austrian throne. The Austro-Hungarian Empire had been looking for an opportunity to extend its authority over Serbia, and Ferdinand's assassination supplied an excuse. When Austria-Hungary declared war on Serbia, various treaties quickly pulled Russia, Germany, France, and Britain into the conflict, and World War I began. Although he had just avoided serving in the Austrian army, Hitler was overjoyed by the opportunity to serve his beloved Germany and immediately volunteered. He entered as a private in the German army; he was later promoted to corporal and received two Iron Crosses for bravery.

The war lasted for four long years, and it used up more and more of Europe's resources. Ordinary citizens suffered because food and supplies were severely rationed. On many school mornings, Viktor Frankl got out of bed at three a.m. in the cold winter darkness. He dressed hurriedly and ran down into the street to stand in a line of other hungry people who waited to buy bread, flour, or whatever

Adolf Hitler (enlarged in the inset) attends a 1914 rally in Munich, celebrating Germany's entry into World War I.

was available. After four hours of standing in the cold, he was always glad to see his mother coming down the sidewalk to take his place in the line so he could run off to school.

During the war, the only vacations the Frankl family could afford were short trips to Porolitz. There, Viktor, his brother, Walter, and their cousin Fritz liked to run and play in the fields outside town. Sometimes they would stand at the edge of a cornfield, their stomachs growling and churning, hungrily eyeing the tall stalks of corn. Looking over their shoulders to make sure no one was watching, they couldn't help grabbing an ear. Then they would run off to fill their rumbling bellies.

Near the end of the war, the need for food was so great that once, when the Frankls received an extra ration coupon, Viktor crossed the Danube River to get a half a cup of flour. As he started across the Reichs Bridge, he found himself surrounded by five tough-looking boys. Menacingly, they sneered and asked, "Are you Jewish?"

Viktor felt they were about to use his heritage as an excuse to attack him. He replied with his own question, "Yes, but does this mean I am not also a human being?" It's impossible to know what went through the other boys' minds when this small, lone boy spoke up with respect for himself and them, but they walked away without hurting him. Later, Viktor said, "It was a human appeal to their own humanness, . . . making them immediately conscious of their responsibility to behave . . . in a human way."

Viktor turned thirteen six months before the end of World War I. It was the year for his bar mitzvah celebration, the traditional Jewish ceremony marking a boy's entry into adulthood. By this time, Viktor had already started attending Sperlgymnasium, the same high school his father had gone to. Throughout junior high, he had been an honor-roll student, but when he entered high school, he started to spend more time on the things he was interested in, mainly psychology and philosophy, and sometimes his grades suffered because of it.

Whenever he could, Viktor used what he had learned about psychology for school papers and presentations. One day in class, he turned off the lights and darkened the windows of the classroom. His teacher and classmates waited with interest. Experience had taught them to expect the unexpected whenever Viktor Frankl had a report to deliver, and he wasn't about to disappoint them this time. His report was about Galvanic Skin Response (GSR), a new discovery in experimental psychology. GSR measures a person's emotional response by monitoring electrical changes in the skin. Scientists had found that when someone has a strong emotional response, it can be measured using a galvanometer attached to the person's skin. A strong response causes a needle on the meter to rise.

Suspense mounted as Viktor attached galvanometer contacts to a friend who had innocently volunteered for the experiment. Viktor set up a projector to display the meter onto the classroom wall. Then, slyly, he said his friend's girlfriend's name. The needle on the wall leaped, because of his classmate's very emotional response. It is easy to imagine the laughter and teasing that followed. Later, Viktor wrote that his friend was lucky, because "the classroom was too dark to see him blush."

Viktor's voracious reading about philosophy and psychology introduced him to the theories of Sigmund Freud, a neurologist and the founder of *psychoanalysis*, a method for investigating and treating emotional and mental problems. Freud developed psychoanalysis at a time when mental patients were still locked away in asylums, and psychiatrists thought that listening to them made their problems worse. By contrast, the main technique of psychoanalysis was listening to patients say whatever came into their minds. From hearing his patients, Freud came to believe that most of human behavior is motivated by unconscious sexual needs and desires. At the time, many people, including other psychologists, were disturbed by his idea that all humans, including infants, have sexual feelings. But Freud's ideas made Viktor quite popular with the boys at Sperlgymnasium. They were naturally curious about any theory having to do with sex, so they were eager to listen to him.

While Viktor's friends went to the Prater park to play soccer or stroll arm in arm with girls, Viktor loved to sit on a bench and grab the attention of a friend to talk about ideas. With World War I over, it was an exciting time to be in Vienna. In a city sometimes called the birthplace of the Modern Age, many people who would later be world famous were experimenting with theories in art, music, architecture, economics, medicine, physics, literature, psychology, and philosophy. Viktor took advantage of all he could and wanted to test these innovative ideas with others. He filled notebook after notebook with the concepts he gathered, many of them about the relationship between philosophy and psychology. One of his teachers started calling him "Mr. Philosopher."

The Riesenrad Ferris wheel in Prater Park.

Despite his scholarly interests, or maybe because he was so absorbed in them, Viktor was often tardy to class. One day, he discovered that he could use psychology and a little wordplay on his teacher to avoid trouble. He rushed into the classroom, late once again. Rapidly, he fired the words, "Please excuse me, sir. I know I am late. But you see, it is because I am not on time, and that is why I am tardy once more." He used all his acting skills as if he were sincerely regretful and as if he were giving a real reason for being late. The teacher barely listened to his words and sent him to his seat without any punishment. Since it worked so well, Viktor used this strategy quite often.

While he had fun and absorbed all he could about his favorite subjects, Viktor was already thinking about the meaning of life, the subject that would lie at the heart of his lifework. One day in science class, the teacher proclaimed, "Life is nothing more than a combustion process, a process of oxidation."

Viktor leaped from his seat and said, "Sir, if this is so, then what can be the meaning of life?" He felt strongly that if life was to be worthwhile, it must have far more meaning than that of a simple process of using and releasing energy. At the same time, like many teens his age, he had entered a struggle with his own doubts about the value of a human life, about what makes us human. He went through a dark period, wondering if his science teacher might be right. He asked himself if it was possible that there is no greater meaning in life than that we are here and then we die.

Viktor sometimes attended adult education courses in the evenings. When he was fifteen or sixteen, he gave a presentation in one of his classes. His talk was on the meaning of life. Even though he was then having some pessimistic thoughts on the subject, his lecture in no way suggested that life might be meaningless. Rather, he presented two ideas that would later be fundamental to his theory of logotherapy. First, he said that it is life that asks something special of each of us human beings, not we who ask life for meaning. In other words, what we give to life, not what we take from it, makes our lives meaningful. Second, Viktor said, "Ultimate meaning is, and must remain, beyond our comprehension." He gave this ultimate meaning the name *suprameaning*, or meaning that is above or beyond everyday meaning.

By the time Viktor turned fifteen, Sigmund Freud had been nominated twice for a Nobel Prize in the category of "Physiology or Medicine." Viktor had already read much of his work, and, unintimidated by Freud's fame, he began to write letters to the psychoanalyst and to send him articles he thought would be of interest to him. Each time he received something, Freud sent Viktor a postcard in response.

At seventeen, Viktor's favorite place to work and study was the Prater. Whenever he was given a writing assignment, he picked a topic that interested him, even if the subject wasn't taught at the Sperlgymnasium. Most often, he researched and wrote about some aspect of psychology. Once he sent an essay he had written in the park to Freud, thinking Freud might find it interesting. Viktor was very surprised when Freud wrote back that he hoped Viktor wouldn't object, but he had sent the article to his own *International Journal of Psychoanalysis* for publication. The class essay Viktor had written at seventeen was published in the professional journal in 1924, when he was nineteen.

As he reached new heights intellectually, Viktor was introduced to heights of another kind. He had never been very interested in sports, but one day a high school friend took him to a rock quarry. His friend was

Sigmund Freud, in the 1920s. At the age of twenty, Viktor met Freud on the street and introduced himself. Freud responded, "Just a minute," then rattled off Viktor's address, which he knew by heart from their frequent correspondence.

a mountain climber and wanted to practice his skills by scaling the sheer rock face of the quarry, and he needed someone to help him with the ropes.

Viktor immediately loved the challenge of conquering any fears that arose as he met a rock wall with his body and tested his limits. He relished the teamwork on which his life and the lives of his companions depended, and he thrilled at the ever-present risks as he used his legs and especially his upper body to move higher and higher. He found that he thrived on the essential, intense concentration that erased thoughts of everything else from his mind, and he developed a profound connection with the rocks themselves. He said, "I fell in love with the walls, the rocks. I *loved* them. I was related to the rocks." Viktor Frankl had found his sport.

At the end of high school, Viktor had to take the Matura exams.

Viktor (far left) in his twenties, with his mountain-climbing companions from the Donauland Alpine Club.

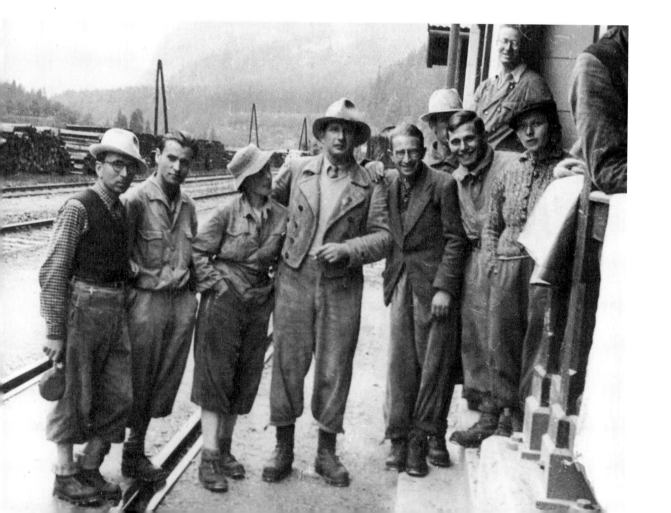

These exams were so difficult that Freud, who had also attended Sperlgymnasium, called them "the martyrdom." In fact, the pressure of the Matura, which qualified students for entry into university, was so great that it was one of the causes of the high teen suicide rate in Vienna. Viktor did well on the exams, though, and was accepted for entrance into the University of Vienna Medical School in the fall of 1924.

As Viktor Frankl prepared to enter medical school, Adolf Hitler, now thirty-five, was serving a jail sentence in the town of Landsberg, fewer than three hundred miles north of Vienna. Germany had lost World War I and had been forced to sign a harsh and humiliating treaty with England, France, and the United States in 1919. The treaty left the country with huge war debts, which, along with the cost of rebuilding the land and cities, plunged German citizens into deep poverty. Millions, a third of the country's workforce, could not find jobs, and there was not enough food.

Many Austrians and Germans, including Hitler, blamed the Jews for Germany's defeat. They accused the Jews of not fighting for Germany and said that those who had been in the army had had easy jobs behind the front. They also believed that Jews had gotten rich from selling goods to the armed forces. In reality, ninety-six thousand Jews fought honorably in World War I on behalf of Germany and Austria, and twelve thousand of them died on the battlefields. Hitler's blind hatred of the Jews caused him to ignore these facts, and he used people's intense feelings about losing the war to build his case against the Jewish race.

After the war, in 1919, Hitler joined the German Workers' Party, which he had been covering as a reporter for the Press and Propaganda Office of the army. He rose quickly in the party and attracted large crowds to his speeches in local beer halls.

In 1920, Hitler spoke on the topic "Why Are We Anti-Semites?"

at a large public meeting. In this speech, he insisted that Jews must be removed from the German nation. At another time, he declared, "The state is a means to an end. Its end lies in the preservation . . . of a community of physically and psychically homogeneous creatures. . . ." In other words, he believed that the whole purpose of a government was to ensure racial purity. To Hitler, the only pure race was the so-called Aryan race—blond, blue-eyed "super people." He said that Germany's future greatness depended on racial purity, and the Jews were the greatest threat to that purity. Others who were "different," like Roma, homosexuals, and Slavs, were also a threat, but Jews were the worst. He repeatedly referred to them as "carriers of filth and disease."

SA members marching in Munich in 1922.

Just two years after Hitler joined the German Workers' Party,

he became its leader. The party name was changed to *Nationalsozialistische Deutsche Arbeiterpartei*, known as the NSDAP, or the Nazis. Hitler began building a private army of men with a taste for violence and intimidation. The group was called the *Sturmabteilung* (meaning storm troopers and abbreviated as SA). The members were also known as Brownshirts because of the color of their uniforms, which included high black boots and red armbands bearing the Nazi swastika. Hitler used the SA, which grew to a paramilitary force of four hundred thousand, to bully ordinary citizens as well as high government officials into following the dictates of the Nazi party. They beat people, destroyed property, and resorted to torture to accomplish their goals.

In 1923 in Munich, Hitler and his "army" tried unsuccessfully to take over the government of Bavaria, an independently ruled region in southeastern Germany. Some of his men were killed in the attempt, and Hitler was arrested and convicted of high treason, which was punishable by life imprisonment; however, he was given only a five-year prison sentence. He served fewer than nine months of the sentence in the Landsberg jail, and while he was there, he wrote the first volume of *Mein Kampf (My Struggle)*. The book was a mixture of self-glorifying autobiography and a diatribe of his social and political ideas, which would later destroy so many lives.

T W O

STANDING ON THE SHOULDERS OF GIANTS

Even though Viktor Frankl first started talking about becoming a doctor when he was three years old, as he learned more about the world, he couldn't help thinking of other possibilities. His friends talked of adventure on the high seas as ships' cabin boys or on the battlefield as army officers. Viktor still wanted to be a doctor, so he extended their fantasies and made them his own. A cabin boy became a ship's doctor, and an army officer, an army doctor. As he matured, his interest in psychoanalysis and psychological research helped him focus his dreams, and he thought maybe he would eventually become a psychiatrist. But in medical school, Viktor learned about other specialties, and it was hard to decide among them. For a while, he thought maybe he would specialize in obstetrics or dermatology.

It was a fellow medical student who helped Viktor make up his mind. He told Viktor that his real gift was in psychiatry and quoted the famous Danish philosopher Søren Kierkegaard to make his point: "Don't despair at wanting to become your authentic self." He was using the quote to tell Viktor that his authentic, or real, self was not an obstetrician or a dermatologist and that he needed to give up those ideas and become a psychiatrist. When Viktor Frankl looked back at this moment, he wrote, "It is difficult to believe what decisive turns in our lives we sometimes owe to even casual remarks made by another person." The remark had touched him deeply; from then on, he knew that he would pursue psychiatry.

In medical school, Viktor studied all areas of medicine, including general surgery. The first time he observed an operation, he had to leave the operating room because he felt as if he would faint. Later, performing brain surgery became one of the four activities he found most exciting. (The others were mountain climbing, casino gambling, and taking a completed book manuscript to his publisher.)

The year he started medical school, Viktor wrote to Sigmund Freud to see if he could join the Vienna Psychoanalytic Society. Even though Viktor was only nineteen, Freud was impressed with him from their correspondence and the article he had published in his journal. He arranged an interview for Viktor with one of his followers, Paul Federn. The interview went well, but Federn suggested that Viktor complete medical school before trying to join the society. Federn also told him that before he could join, he would have to complete many months of psychoanalysis as a patient.

In classical Freudian psychoanalysis, a patient often spent several hours a week with the psychoanalyst. The person lay on a couch and spoke whatever thoughts came into his mind. The idea was that in doing this, the patient and doctor would deeply probe the patient's unconscious mind and uncover the motivations underlying his behavior and feelings. Federn felt that the psychoanalytic process would distract Viktor from his medical studies and that he might end up with more mental problems than when he started. He said, "After all, if you are lying down on a couch for years, and if you don't have problems, you *create* them!"

Even though he had wanted to join the Psychoanalytic Society, Viktor was becoming critical of psychoanalysis. After his interview with Federn, he decided that psychoanalysis was not really a science. He thought that if it were a science, he should be able to rationally examine its principles one by one and accept or reject them based on his investigation. He was beginning to get the impression that the members of the Psychoanalytic Society didn't encourage scrutiny and free discussion of its theories. Rather, he would be forced to go through years of analysis before he had enough information to make a decision about its validity.

Viktor saw another major problem with psychoanalysis. He felt that human beings and their behaviors are very complex. In high school, Viktor had known intuitively that his science teacher was wrong to reduce life to a simple exchange of energy. At nineteen, he saw that psychoanalysis reduced the complexities of being human to a single mechanism of unconscious drives. He felt that such a reduction was incorrect.

When Viktor found that psychoanalysis did not satisfy his need to understand human nature, he looked for other people who might be thinking about these questions in different ways. Alfred Adler was an ophthalmologist who had become interested in psychoanalysis and was one of Freud's early followers. However, he had separated from Freud in 1911 because he believed that social influences have a greater effect on human development than unconscious drives do. For example, Adler thought that when children are treated badly by their parents or peers, they develop inferiority complexes; that is, they feel that they aren't as good as other people. Based on this thinking, Adler founded his own method of psychology and named it *social psychology*. He believed that the job of psychotherapists was to help people, and especially children, overcome their feelings of inferiority.

Adler and his followers, who became known as Adlerians, set up child guidance clinics in Vienna and many other places in the world. Their goal was to help children and youths with their problems. One way they did that was to try to create change in the educational system so it would support children to develop as healthy human beings. In his last year of high school, Viktor visited some of the guidance clinics and through his visits was introduced to Adler himself. He began to meet with Adler and the Adlerians at the doctor's favorite café. It just happened to be the Café Siller—the coffeehouse that had almost been Viktor's birthplace.

Alfred Adler aboard the ship that took him from Europe to the United States to lecture at Columbia University in 1933.

A year after his first article was published in Freud's journal, Viktor chose social psychology (also known as *individual psychology*) over psychoanalysis. Even though he was a busy student at one of the leading medical schools in the world, Viktor found time to expand his ideas and experience in the area of psychology. Drs. Rudolf Allers and Oswald Schwarz were members of Adler's group. Viktor began to work with Allers on the doctor's research on the physiology of the senses. Schwarz was pioneering a field he named *psychosomatic medicine*, studying the interdependence of mind and body. Viktor worked with him, too, and began to think of him as his mentor.

Café Siller, with its large white window awnings, is immediately to the left of Ferdinand's Bridge.

Viktor became an active member of the Adlerian group in 1925, and he made a name for himself with them as quickly as he had with the Freudians. A year after his article was published in Freud's journal, another article of his appeared in Adler's journal. But, just as he had criticized Freud earlier, Viktor had begun to see weaknesses in Adler's theories. He observed that, like Freud, Adler reduced the human experience to a single motivation. While Freud thought that unconscious sexual and aggressive drives dictated human behavior, Adler thought the need for social superiority was its motivating force. Both Freud and Adler explained human behavior in terms of emotional problems rather than emotional health.

When he was just twenty-one, Viktor was honored with an invitation to present the keynote address at the International Congress for Individual Psychology in Düsseldorf, Germany. In his speech, Frankl came out and said that he believed that not all human behavior was motivated by illness. He stated that some behaviors might look like the symptoms of illness but could actually be expressions of one's innermost being, one's true self. For example, someone who showed symptoms of depression might actually be expressing dissatisfaction with her life, a need to find a more meaningful career. Even though the depression looked like illness, Frankl would say that in this case the depressed person was expressing her true self, or a need to express herself more fully. Allers and Schwarz agreed with Viktor that human beings are complex and that a single cause-and-effect relationship, such as the need for superiority, could not explain all behavior. A year after giving his address, Viktor was expelled from the Society for Individual Psychology because he had criticized parts of Adlerian psychology. His mentors, Drs. Allers and Schwarz, were expelled at the same time.

Although he disagreed with Adler on certain points, Viktor was disappointed he could no longer associate with the group and exchange ideas with its members. Furthermore, for a year he had been the editor of an individual psychology journal, *Der Mensch im Alltag* (*The Person in Daily Living*). Being expelled from the society meant giving up his editorship, which was important to him because it gave him a place to express his ideas to others in the field of psychotherapy.

From the day Frankl was expelled, Adler refused to speak to him again, even when he came up to Adler's table at Café Siller and greeted him. Frankl, however, continued to honor both Freud and Adler as the great thinkers they were. He thought of them as the men who had provided him with the foundations for his own development in the field of psychiatry. Regarding their influence on him, Viktor said, "Even a dwarf standing on the shoulders of a giant can see farther." To Viktor, Freud and Adler were the giants on whose shoulders he had stood to get his first glimpses of psychotherapy; they had enabled him to move on and develop his own principles of therapy. At one time, he drew a cartoon, titled "The Three Schools of Viennese Psychotherapy," showing Freud as the largest man, Adler next in size, and himself as the smallest.

While Viktor honored Freud and Adler, he was passionately committed to his own theory and practice of psychology—logotherapy. Since childhood, Viktor had been fascinated with questions about the meaning of life, and he began to formulate the principles of logotherapy while he was still in medical school. The word *logotherapy* comes from two Greek words, *logos* and *therapeia*. One definition for *logos* is *meaning*. *Therapeia* means *therapy* or *treatment*. Logotherapy, then, is the treatment of emotional pain through helping people find meaning in their lives. According to Viktor Frankl, "striving to find a meaning in one's life is the primary motivational force in man."

By the time he was twenty-four, Viktor had developed the concept that there are three main ways of finding meaning in life. The first is through action or creation. An example of *meaning through action* might be an auto mechanic who feels her life is meaningful when she comes up with the correct diagnosis for an ailing car and then repairs it. *Meaning through creation* can occur when a musician finds satisfaction in writing and recording a piece of music.

Viktor's cartoon "The Three Schools of Viennese Psychotherapy."

The second way to find meaning, Frankl said, is through an experience, a human encounter, or love. An example of *meaning through experience* might be the exhilaration of scaling a difficult mountain face, as Viktor himself experienced. *Meaning through a human encounter* might occur through something as simple as an exchange of smiles with a stranger on the street. *Meaning through love* can be experienced in countless ways, such as romantic love, love for family members, and love for friends.

The third path to meaning, *meaning through suffering*, can come about when a person responds to a difficult or even fatal life situation that is outside his or her control. Viktor called this the "ability to turn suffering into human triumph." For example, a teenager who faces living with alcoholic parents can get lost in the pain of that life and let it destroy his possibilities for happiness. Or he can choose to focus on achieving his own life goals, on creating a better and happier life for himself. Viktor would later turn his own suffering in the concentration camps into a triumph that not only enabled him to survive but also helped many others meet their own fates courageously.

Viktor Frankl's logotherapy was the beginning of what would later be known among psychotherapists as the *human potential movement*. Freud's psychoanalysis and Adler's individual psychology both emphasize how people's flaws cause them to behave the way they do. Logotherapy, on the other hand, focuses on the possibilities humans can create out of their reality, hence on human *potential*.

After he was expelled from the Adlerian group, Viktor began to think about how he could put his ideas to practical use. The rate of teen suicide was very high in Vienna. Students felt a lot of pressure to succeed, and many suicides occurred when high school report cards came out. Many young people were also depressed or anxious about sexual conflicts. For example, many were upset about the clash between their own feelings about masturbation and what their parents or the church had taught them. Viktor organized youth counseling centers, first in Vienna and later in six other cities in Europe. He got psychiatrists, physicians, psychologists, and clergy to volunteer their time. Schedules for free drop-in times were posted throughout the city. Many well-known professionals in Vienna volunteered. Several of them were Adlerians who did not feel the same animosity toward Viktor as Adler did. By the second year of the counseling centers' existence, and for the first time in history, no student suicides were reported in Vienna.

Viktor himself held office hours at the Frankl family apartment from three to four p.m. on Saturdays, and on weekday afternoons in an office owned by the city of Vienna. He found that, in addition to being affected by social pressures, some of the young people he worked with were depressed because they couldn't find work. They felt that they were useless if they didn't have jobs. Viktor listened kindly to his patients talk about their feelings of worthlessness, and then he responded with the caring toughness that would become a hallmark of logotherapy. Rather than comforting them, Viktor let his young patients know that life asked something of them and that they had a responsibility to respond. Although it can be very hard for someone to take action when he is depressed, Viktor recommended that the youths find places to volunteer in their communities. Once they were engaged in meaningful activities, even if they weren't paid, their depression often was relieved.

Viktor received his medical doctor (MD) degree in 1930, after six years of schooling. He went on to do hospital internships and residencies in neurology and psychiatry in several hospitals and clinics. His last assignment as a resident was at the very modern Steinhof Psychiatric Hospital, designed by the renowned architect Otto Wagner. The church that was part of the hospital had been planned and built with mental patients in mind. Some of its features included rounded furniture to prevent injury, in case a

A 1936 Viennese high school class with its teacher.

patient became violent, and attached rooms where the staff could take patients who needed immediate treatment. Viktor felt that the "awe-inspiring building soothed and lifted the spirits of patients, even those severely troubled."

At Steinhof, Viktor was responsible for the treatment of approximately three thousand patients a year, most of them suicidal women. He decided he needed to forget whatever he had learned from Freud and Adler and simply listen to what his patients were telling him. When he worked with a depressed woman who had been in the hospital for a few days, he would ask if she still had ideas about committing suicide. If the woman said no, he asked more questions. He wanted to make sure she had really changed her mind and wasn't saying no just so she could be discharged from the

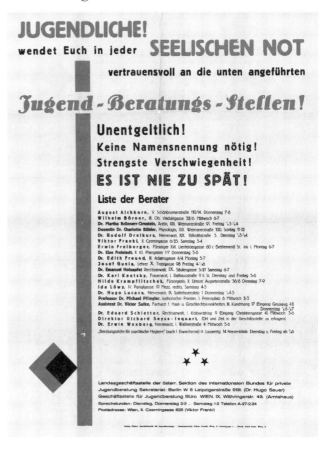

A poster for the Youth Counseling Centers founded by Frankl. Volunteer counselors are listed in alphabetical order, with Viktor's name appearing sixth on the list. The poster encourages young people to seek help: "It's never too late!"

hospital to go out and actually kill herself. So he asked why she no longer felt she wanted to commit suicide. If she gave him reasons, such as wanting to live for her children, needing to follow her religious beliefs, or wanting to complete a project, Frankl knew that she was on her way to recovery. If she answered with an embarrassed silence, he knew that she had still not decided that her life was worth living. He said, "I knew that if there was meaning to their lives, these patients would become free from suicide."

Viktor's patients often delighted his sense of humor, and he filled a notebook with curious things they said. One day he saw a patient walking barefoot, carrying his shoes. Viktor asked him why he was carrying them. Maybe he expected the patient's answer to have something to do with his mental illness. But the patient replied, "Why not? After all, they're not very heavy." Dr. Frankl observed that, despite their illness, what his patients said often made perfect sense.

Viktor's sense of humor helped him look at things with fresh eyes and create new ways of helping his patients with their problems. He developed a rather humorous yet very effective approach to obsessive, irrational fears. He named the approach *paradoxical intention*. Paradoxical intention can best be explained by an example. A person who perspired heavily in public might begin to focus obsessively on his perspiration, getting more and more nervous about it. His nervousness would make him sweat more and more. Then he would fear going out in public because he would expect to get embarrassing patches of sweat under his arms, on his back, on his face.

Dr. Frankl would suggest a paradoxical intention: instead of being afraid of sweating and trying to avoid it by not going out, the patient should imagine himself going out and purposely perspiring an exaggerated amount. He should see himself pouring sweat into gallon buckets, wringing the sweat out of his clothing by the cupful. This paradoxical intention, or moving toward what a person feared, rather than running from it, most often had the effect of curing the person of his or her obsession.

Viktor loved to tell the story of how he once used paradoxical intention with a police officer to get out of a speeding ticket. An officer pulled him over and walked up to his window with a scowl, addressing him in a menacing tone. Instead of making excuses and trying to get out of the ticket, Viktor immediately began to accuse himself of wrongdoing. "You're right, officer. How could I do such a thing? I have no excuse. I am sure I will never do it again, and this will be a lesson to me. This is certainly a crime that deserves punishment." In the same way that a patient was advised to trick his own mind with the unusual exaggeration of the thing he feared, Viktor tricked the mind of the police officer by begging for punishment instead of trying to get out of it. The scene ended with the officer comforting Viktor. He told Viktor sympathetically that it could happen to anyone and drove off without giving him a ticket.

While Viktor gave his patients at Steinhof the priceless gift of listening to them with compassion and respect mixed with humor and firmness, many of them, without knowing it, also gave him a gift. Mental patients often do not have the inhibitions, or social

The church at Steinhof Psychiatric Hospital was constructed with the needs of mental patients in mind.

self-control, that most of us are taught to have. In polite 1930s society, people who were anti-Semitic usually had the self-control not to speak their prejudices openly. But when Viktor made his hospital rounds, many patients would shout insults at him: "Again this dirty Jewish swine is coming!" Viktor heard these things so often that he began to develop an immunity that would help him later on.

THRee

HITLER COMES TO POWER

In November 1924, a few months after Viktor started medical school, Adolf Hitler was released from the Landsberg prison. Upon his release, he decided to use the political process rather than military force to gain power. That year, the Nazi party won thirty-two seats in the German *Reichstag* (parliament), five percent of the total number of seats. The 1929 American stock market crash, which started a worldwide economic depression, increased Nazi popularity in Germany because Hitler placed a strong emphasis on addressing the country's economic problems. In 1930, the Nazis won 107 seats, 18 percent of all the seats, in the Reichstag. The party continued to grow, and in 1932, Hitler ran for president of Germany against Paul von Hindenburg, the aging incumbent. Hindenburg won, with nineteen million votes, but Hitler, who campaigned far more vigorously than Hindenberg, was close behind with thirteen million. That same year, the Nazi party became the largest party in Germany, winning 230 seats (37 percent of all the seats in the Reichstag).

In 1933, the year Viktor Frankl began his final residency at Steinhof, President Hindenburg, against his own wishes, appointed Hitler chancellor of Germany. Under the German constitution, the president served as a balancing force among the various branches of government, but the chancellor had the greatest power. Hindenburg did not especially disagree with Hitler's policies, but he did not respect him, because Hitler was an Austrian and not from the elite upper class. However, because Germany's previous chancellors had been unable to rectify the country's economic situation, and because Hitler had won such a high percentage of the popular vote, Hindenburg was pressured from many sides to choose him.

Hitler lost no time securing dictatorial powers for himself. He had an ingenious plan that would grant him these powers legally. Because the Nazi party still did not hold a majority in the Reichstag, Hitler needed to form a coalition with other parties. Secretly pitting possible allies against each other, he informed President von Hindenberg that a coalition was impossible; therefore, the Reichstag would need to be dissolved and new elections held. Despite heavy Nazi campaigning, backed by the resources of government and industry, 56 percent of the German population voted against Hitler on March 5, 1933. Nevertheless, the Nazis now held 44 percent of the Reichstag seats; when they added the Nationalist representatives, who supported them, they had a slim majority of 52 percent.

Since Hitler's plan for gaining total control of the government involved changing the constitution, he needed a two-thirds majority. He ordered the SA to begin terrorizing and arresting Communist and Socialist Reichstag members, who would have formed the strongest opposition to his plan. With all the Communists and twenty-six Socialists missing, Hitler got the Reichstag to vote away its own power by passing the Enabling Act. With only ninety-four Social Democrats voting against it, the Enabling Act was approved on March 23, 1933. The act made Hitler dictator for the next four years, giving him the power even to make decisions that contradicted the constitution if he thought those decisions were in the best interests of the country. In the years that followed, Hitler would use his position to renew the act whenever necessary. He was to be known from then on as the *Führer*, meaning *leader*—in this case, *supreme leader*. The new German government was named the *Third Reich* and was expected to last for a thousand years.

Hitler receiving an ovation in the Reichstag. The raised arms are the "Heil Hitler" salute, which until the end of World War II became a nearly universal greeting in Germany and the countries it conquered.

Two days earlier, one of Hitler's highest officials, Heinrich Himmler, had announced the creation of Dachau, the first Nazi concentration camp. He stated that its purpose was to restrict "all Communist and, where necessary, *Reichsbanner* [the Social Democrats' paramilitary organization] and Social Democrat officials . . . [who] cannot be allowed to remain free as they continue to agitate and to cause unrest." Most countries in the Western world saw Communism and Socialism as grave threats to economic and political freedom and did not object to the idea that these elected officials would be placed in a prison camp.

During the next four years, while Viktor completed his final psychiatric training, Hitler enacted one law after another, taking away the rights of Jews in Germany. As all medical residents are, Viktor was extremely busy, absorbed in his work. Besides being a medical resident, he continued to coordinate the teen-suicide counseling program and to speak about it in other countries. He also wrote articles about neurology and psychiatry and continued to develop the principles of logotherapy. In his spare time, he pursued his other great passion, mountain climbing. He didn't have time or energy to give very much attention to politics and to what Hitler was doing in Germany, but as a Central European Jew living in Hitler's homeland, he couldn't help being aware of the actions of Germany's new dictator. And he couldn't help thinking that this man's actions might some day affect him.

When Viktor finished his residency in 1937, he opened a private practice in neurology and psychiatry in his sister Stella's living room. His brother, Walter, designed a special desk with built-in bookshelves for his new office, and Viktor began seeing patients. His practice represented a new beginning, an exhilarating outcome after years of hard work. However, it was to have a very short life.

Austria was the first country Hitler hoped to include in his new

German empire. Soon after he became chancellor of Germany, he began to make demands on the Austrian government. At the time, the Nazi party was outlawed in Austria, and a number of party members were in prison. Hitler's first demand was that they be granted amnesty. He threatened a military invasion if his requirements were not met. Because the demand also guaranteed Austria's sovereignty, Austria's chancellor Schuschnigg agreed.

In February 1938, Hitler increased his demands, insisting that even the Nazis who had assassinated Schuschnigg's predecessor, Engelbert Dollfuss, be released and that the Nazi party be legalized. This time, he presented his ultimatum to Schuschnigg in person, also requiring him to install several Nazis in key positions in his government, which amounted to doing away with Austria's sovereignty. Once again, Hitler backed his demands with the threat of an invasion. Schuschnigg tried to resist by calling for a vote on the demands, hoping to gain the support of the Austrian people. At this point, Hitler began to mobilize German troops at the German-Austrian border, raising the stakes further. The vote was scheduled for March 13.

On Friday, March 11, 1938, tension was building in Vienna. In desperation, Schuschnigg appealed to the Social Democrats, whose party he had previously suppressed. The Nazis, Social Democrats, and others both for and against Austrian inde-

A streetcar with an advertisement for a speech to be given by German Reich minister Rudolf Hess in favor of the annexation of Austria by Germany.

pendence put up posters and made speeches over loudspeakers, competing for the citizens' votes. Behind the scenes, Germany put intense pressure on Chancellor Schuschnigg to cancel the vote. Based on several careful observations, William Shirer, an American journalist in Vienna, believed that with the support of the Social Democrats, Schuschnigg would have won the vote. As the pressure increased, Schuschnigg began to capitulate. At six-fifteen p.m., the radio announced that the vote would be postponed indefinitely.

A psychiatrist from the University of Vienna Psychiatric Clinic had asked Viktor if he would substitute for him that evening as a lecturer at the Urania Theater. The scheduled topic was "Nervousness as a Phenomenon of Our Time." Viktor agreed to speak. The Urania is on the Ringstrasse, a street that encircles the center of Vienna and has on it many grand public buildings. On his way to the theater, Viktor was jostled by excited people who were crowding into the Ring. The postponement of the vote meant to many relieved Viennese citizens that Germans troops would be taking over Austria without military action. In a broadcast from London the next day, William Shirer noted that following the radio announcement, the opponents to unification with Germany disappeared from the streets and were replaced by tens of thousands of jubilant Nazis, many of whom had taken brown and black shirts out of storage (he said the shirts smelled of mothballs) and put on the Nazi armband. They had been hoping for the day when all German-speaking people would be united. Now their slogan, "One Reich, one people, one leader," was becoming a reality.

Despite the charged atmosphere and possible danger, Viktor proceeded to the theater. On the Ringstrasse, the mood was one of excitement, not nervousness, the subject of Viktor's lecture. But Vienna's Jews and anyone else who opposed Nazism certainly had reason to be worried. Vienna had a long tradition of anti-Semitism toward its Jewish citizens. Jews were not allowed to be members of certain social clubs; newspapers, posters, and jokes portrayed them in degrading ways; the Catholic Church, a powerful force in Vienna, condemned Jews as Christ-killers. It was reasonable to fear that the anti-Jewish laws already on the books in Germany would quickly be enacted in Austria after the expected German takeover.

Viktor had been speaking for a while when suddenly one of the auditorium's doors flew open. A storm trooper in full uniform planted himself in the entrance. Viktor expected the SA officer to close down the lecture and order everyone home. In a split second, he decided he would do everything in his power to keep that from happening. Whenever he spoke, Viktor engaged his audience with lively movements, an energetic voice, and stories from life. Now he launched himself into his most animated speaking style and managed to turn the tables on the Brownshirt standing there. For the next half hour, Viktor Frankl held the man captive with his words. Frankl said later, "He did not make a move to interrupt me."

The Urania Theater, pictured here, is where Viktor Frankl lectured on the eve of the Anschluss. It is the building with the round-roofed tower immediately to the left of the Aspern Bridge.

When Viktor walked out of the Urania, the streets had been transformed into a sea of people, and many were waving burning torches. They yelled, "Down with the Jews! Heil Hitler! Hang Schuschnigg!" While Viktor had been lecturing about anxiety, Chancellor Schuschnigg had given his resignation speech on Austrian radio. Jews and intellectuals stayed in their homes while the crowds in the streets went wild. When Viktor got home, his mother was crying for fear of what was to come.

On Saturday, March 12, German troops began to pour into Austria in tanks and trucks and on foot. People lined the streets, cheering and throwing flowers. Those who welcomed Hitler believed that this was the beginning of the German empire they had dreamed of. In Vienna, people waited to receive him into the city he had slunk away from in defeat in 1913. But Hitler was waiting to hear from the Austrian *Parlament* (parliament). He wanted them to pass a law allowing Germany to annex, or add, Austria to Germany without a war. On Sunday he got the news he was waiting for, and on Monday, March 14, Hitler made his triumphal entry into Vienna. He stayed in the Imperial Hotel, where he had shoveled snow twenty-five years earlier. There, he stood on the balcony of the royal suite beneath a sculpture of Emperor Franz Josef surrounded by lions and stags. He waved to the excited crowds below. The following day he gave a victory speech at the *Heldenplatz* (Heroes' Square) to many thousands of rejoicing Austrians. The annexation of Austria by Germany is known as the *Anschluss*.

As many had expected, anti-Semitism became the law. Vienna's Jews were publicly humiliated. Hundreds of adults, some of them famous, were forced to scrub the sidewalks and buildings. Children were forced at gunpoint to paint the word *Jude* (Jew) on their parents' store windows. One girl had to wear a sign that read, "Do not buy from me. I am a Jewish sow." Jews as well as known anti-Nazis were stripped of their property and businesses, and many were deported to Dachau and another camp called Buchenwald.

Viktor discovered that the anti-Semitic insults some of his mental patients had shouted at him on the hospital wards were now surprisingly helpful to him. When passersby shouted out their anti-Semitic prejudices in the streets, he found himself thinking, "This is just another psychotic person." Viktor's ability to look at things from a novel perspective had turned his former patients' insults into a gift that helped him survive shameful treatment with dignity.

On October 6, 1938, three of Vienna's synagogues were destroyed by fire. On November 9 and 10, throughout Germany and Austria, there was a rampage of anti-Jewish destruction. More than a hundred Viennese synagogues and Jewish prayer houses were demolished. Windows were broken, and businesses and homes set on fire. These two nights became known as *Kristallnacht* (Crystal Night), because the shards of broken glass glittered in the firelit nights like pieces of crystal.

After the Nazi takeover of Austria, Jewish children were no longer allowed to attend public school, and Jewish professionals—

Viennese Nazis and other citizens look on as Jewish citizens are forced to scrub the pavement immediately after the Anschluss.

teachers, doctors, lawyers—were stripped of their credentials. All Jews were forced to wear a six-pointed yellow star on their clothing, identifying them as Jews. They were not allowed to use public transportation. Jewish men had to add the name Israel, and women the name Sarah, to their official papers.

Viktor lost his hard-won medical license. His sister's apartment, including his office and custom-built desk, was given to an "Aryan" family. He moved his practice to his parents' home, where he was forced to put up a blue sign that read, "Dr. Viktor Emil Israel Frankl, Jew-Caretaker for Neurology and Psychiatry." From then on he could treat only Jewish patients, and he was no longer considered a member of his profession.

After Kristallnacht, many German and Austrian Jews tried every way they could think of to get permission to leave the two countries. Viktor's sister, Stella, and her husband left for Australia, while his brother and sister-in-law, Walter and Else, went to Italy. Viktor

The inside of the synagogue in Hechningen, Germany, the day after it was destroyed on Kristallnacht.

himself applied for a visa to the United States. Jews left for places as far away as China, India, and Kenya to escape the terrors of Nazism. Sigmund Freud, in very poor health by this time, fled to London after storm troopers raided his Vienna home and arrested his daughter. His daughter was released and went with him.

After the easy annexation of Austria, Hitler began vigorously promoting his policy of *Lebensraum* (living space), which he had introduced in *Mein Kampf*. The ideas that the German people needed more living space and that people of German heritage should be united in one country became the excuse for Germany's next annexation. Hitler began to press the Czechoslovakian government to turn over the western side of Czechoslovakia, known as the Sudetenland, which contained about three and a half million ethnic Germans; he threatened a military takeover of the entire country if his demand was not met. Czech leaders appealed to Britain and France for help. Because those countries were trying to avoid another world war at all costs, rather than come to Czechoslovakia's defense, they engineered an agreement in which the Czech government withdrew from the Sudetenland. Soon after that, on the pretext that Germany needed to quell disturbances in the rest of Czechoslovakia, Hitler threatened an armed invasion if Czech President Hacha did not grant Germany control of the whole country. Knowing he had no outside support, Hacha yielded.

Hitler looked next to Poland to increase Germany's holdings. The Treaty of Versailles had granted Poland a corridor of land between western Germany and the part of Germany known as East Prussia. The corridor contained the desirable seaport of Danzig, whose population was mostly German. As he had with Austria and Czechoslovakia, Hitler started with a small demand: Give us back Danzig, and you can continue to use it freely as a port. Poland refused, and both countries made agreements with potential allies in

In a forceful display, SA troops hold hands to prevent Jews from entering a University of Vienna building.

an effort to shore up their positions. Hitler began planning an attack on Poland for September 1, 1939. This time, he fully intended military action, and on August 31, he ordered German commandos disguised as Poles to undertake anti-German actions, thus creating an excuse for the invasion. Britain and France honored the agreements they had made with Poland and declared war on Germany. World War II had begun.

Although Britain and France had declared war, their ground troops could not reach Poland in time to be of use against the rapid advance of the German attack, known as a *Blitzkrieg* (lightning war). They were reluctant to send air support, because they still hoped to avoid a full-scale conflict. However, the Soviet Union, which had signed an agreement with Germany, was ready to assist Hitler and did invade Poland from the east. Poland fought back, but in less than a month, it had been conquered.

Germany was not the only country that sought to add to its land base. In 1937, Germany and Italy had made an agreement to cooperate, or at least not interfere with each other militarily. The two countries formed what was known as the Berlin-Rome Axis. Italy began its land grab by invading Ethiopia, one of its former colonies. In 1940, Germany and Italy were joined by Japan in what was known as the Tripartite Pact. After that, the three countries were called the Axis Powers. By 1941, Hungary and Romania had also become members of the Axis. Together, the Axis Powers took over most of Europe, sometimes even trading off the occupation of different countries among themselves. The countries that opposed the Axis Powers were known as the Allies.

In *Mein Kampf*, Hitler had written, "Germany's final objective must unswervingly be the removal of Jews altogether." When the German army rolled into Poland, *Einsatzgruppen* (Special Duty Groups) accompanied them. The Einsatzgruppen were charged with removing and destroying Jews and forcing Slavs into slave labor. They rounded up Jewish people by the thousands, marched them to ditches that would become mass graves, and shot them. Anyone who tried to escape was shot.

This method of destruction, however, was not fast or efficient enough for Hitler. In the spring of 1941, he set in motion what he called the *Final Solution to the Jewish Question*. It was one of the Third Reich's central policies, and its goal was the total eradication of Jews—first from Germany, then Europe, then the entire world. Heinrich Himmler, described as Hitler's most loyal follower, masterminded the Final Solution, using the SS (*Schutztaffel,* or Guard Squadron), which was under his command. The SS grew from an elite bodyguard corps of two hundred eighty to what amounted to an ancillary government that was more than twenty-five thousand strong. The SS is best known as the arm that created and ran the concentration camps, but it also acted as a police force, a military unit, an agricultural-industrial complex, and a research facility.

Once the Final Solution was put in place, the SS under Himmler and his assistant, Reinhard Heydrich, began furiously enlarging existing concentration camps and building additional ones. Some camps were labor camps, set up to get as much work out of people as possible until they collapsed and died from exhaustion, starvation, and exposure to weather. Other camps were combination labor and death camps. Of these, Auschwitz would become the most well known after the war, in part because of its size. Auschwitz was chosen as an annihilation camp because it was close to a railroad, so people could easily be transported there. It was also isolated and therefore relatively hidden, which was important because the Nazi plan was to keep their extermination of the Jews and others secret from the rest of the world. People arrived at Auschwitz in cattle cars, and when they reached the gates, many were already dead from hunger, exposure, and thirst. When those who were still alive stumbled off the trains, clouds of smoke and the stench of burning flesh greeted them. A Nazi doctor stood on a platform and ordered them to the right or left. Children, the old and infirm, and most women were sent to the left, to immediate death in gas chambers. Those who looked as if they might be able to work were sent to the right, into slave labor. Most often this meant a slow death.

Even when it became clear that the expense of this death machine could cost Germany the war, Hitler continued to order the grim, efficient killing. In the end, six million Jews—two-thirds of Europe's Jewish population—and five million non-Jews were murdered in what has come to be called the Holocaust. The word *holocaust* comes from two Greek words, *olos,* meaning *whole,* and *kaustos,* meaning *burnt.* Originally, it was used to refer to burnt sacrifices. In the nineteenth and early twentieth centuries, writers used

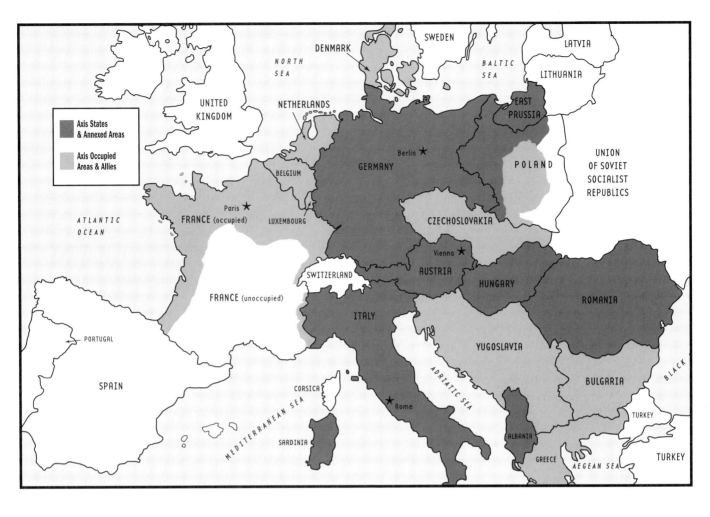

holocaust to describe the mass destruction of human lives by both nature and other humans. Today *holocaust*, with a captial *H*, refers specifically to the destruction of Jews and others at the hands of the Nazis. Its meaning is both literal and figurative, since whole populations were burned in mass cremations, while other methods destroyed millions more.

Occupied Europe, 1941

In the upside-down world of Nazism, while thousands of Jews were taken to the slaughter, there were still Jewish hospitals, dedicated to saving Jewish lives. Although he was no longer considered a physician, in 1940, Viktor Frankl became the chief of neurology at Rothschild, one of the Jewish hospitals. Ever since violence against Jews had become policy in 1938, the hospital had been so full of Jewish wounded that at times they could only be placed in the hallways and on the lawns.

One night while he was working at the Rothschild, Viktor had a dream that moved him deeply. In his dream, a group of mentally ill patients were lined up in front of a gas chamber, waiting their turn to be exterminated. At the time, it was Hitler's policy that doctors in mental hospitals must identify both children and adults considered physically deformed, mentally retarded, or mentally ill. Those patients were then targeted for euthanization, or "mercy killing." The program was stopped, at least officially, in 1940, as the public became more and more aware of it, in part through the efforts of a German Catholic priest, Bishop von Galen.

In Viktor's dream, he watched the line of patients, thought for a moment, then stepped forward to join them. He had heard about a Polish pediatrician, Janusz Korczak, who had voluntarily entered a gas chamber with the children who were in his care. He thought his dream might have been triggered by the story of the brave Polish doctor, since he knew that dreams are often connected with events in our daily lives. But perhaps Viktor also had some sense of what awaited him and of the courage he would show while working in the hospital and also later, on behalf of others in the camps.

While the euthanization program was still in effect, Viktor and a colleague, Dr. Otto Pötzl, collaborated many times to save the lives of Jewish patients. Dr. Pötzl had joined the Nazi party, and while people would later criticize Viktor for working with him, Viktor judged his friend by his actions rather than his party affiliation. Because he was a party member, Pötzl had the power to help Viktor save Jewish lives, and he often risked his own life doing so. He continued to treat Jewish patients, although that was illegal for him as a non-Jewish doctor.

Dr. Pötzl and Viktor worked out a scheme to save Jewish mental patients scheduled for euthanization. When a mental patient came to Dr. Pötzl, he referred the patient to a Jewish home for the aged. Then he notified Viktor of the referral by phone, and Viktor rushed to the nursing home. There he gave the patient a false diagnosis that would allow the person to be hospitalized in a home for elderly Jews rather than in a mental institution. For example, schizophrenic patients were condemned to be gassed as undesirables. Jewish schizophrenics were doubly undesirable. Viktor could give a Jewish schizophrenic a diagnosis of aphasia, the inability to speak, a common symptom in elderly people who have had a stroke. A patient diagnosed as aphasic could be placed in the Jewish home for the aged and thus saved, at least for a while. Pötzl and Frankl could use this strategy only for patients whose symptoms could be controlled enough that they would escape the attention of the authorities.

Because Viktor was the head of a department at the Rothschild Hospital, he and his family were protected for a time from deportation. Then there came a close call in which Viktor's expertise as a psychiatrist kept him and his parents safe from deportation for an

Viktor Frankl (center), the chief of neurology, with colleagues at Rothschild Hospital in 1940. After the Anschluss, only Jewish patients could be treated there.

additional year. That extra year outside the concentration camps may well have saved his life.

Early one morning, the phone rang in the Frankl apartment, and Viktor's mother answered it. With fear in her voice she said, "Viktor, the Gestapo." The Gestapo were the dreaded Nazi secret police.

Viktor picked up the phone. The voice on the other end told him to report at nine the next morning to Gestapo headquarters. Viktor asked, "Shall I bring a second set of clothes?"

"Yes," came the answer. Viktor knew that could mean only one thing: he was headed for a concentration camp.

When he arrived the next morning, Viktor was ushered into an interrogation office. The man behind the desk started asking questions about a spy who had crossed the border into Switzerland. He asked, "Do you know Herzog?"

Viktor had heard the name, but he didn't know the man.

The officer then changed tactics. "How come you have not yet been arrested?"

No one could be sure why some people had been arrested and others hadn't. Viktor thought he was still safe because of his position at the Rothschild Hospital. He said this to the Gestapo man, who kept hammering away with more questions.

"How come your father has not yet been arrested?"

Viktor thought maybe his father was being spared, at least temporarily, because of his thirty-five years as the director of a government department and because of Viktor's position in the hospital.

One of the Gestapo's techniques was to ask question after question until the person being interrogated got tired and started to make mistakes. A mistake became a pretense for an arrest. The man asked, "What is your medical specialty?"

When Viktor told him it was psychiatry, the interview process changed. The Gestapo man seemed to forget that he was there to get information for Viktor's arrest. He started asking questions to satisfy his curiosity about psychotherapy and psychoanalysis. The large hand on the clock made its rounds twice, and then some.

Other Gestapo officers came into the room. Each time one came in, Viktor rose from his seat to show respect. Quite possibly, he thought they were there to arrest him. Each time, the interviewer motioned him to sit again.

Each time an officer left, the interrogator grew more and more relaxed. It was as if he were warming up to the subject he really wanted to talk about. At last, he asked Dr. Frankl, "How do you treat agoraphobia? I have a friend who has agoraphobia. What can I tell him?"

Agoraphobia is an irrational fear of open spaces. People afflicted with agoraphobia are terrified of leaving their homes or familiar enclosed spaces. They are frightened of collapsing and being left helpless in public with no way to get to safety. The fear can cripple them and make it impossible for them to lead a normal life.

Viktor quickly suspected that the real patient was the Gestapo man himself, rather than the man's friend. He told the man about paradoxical intention, but he went along with the man, as if he believed he was trying to help his friend. "Tell him, whenever he has an attack of his phobia, he should say to himself, 'I am afraid I could collapse on the street. Fine then, that is exactly what I want. I will collapse and a crowd will gather around me. Worse than that, I will have a heart attack and a stroke to boot.'"

A smile spread across the man's face. Viktor said, "Tell your friend that when his anxiety crops up, he should go for a walk and try to [have] five strokes, and . . . he will start smiling just as you are smiling, and he will have the victory over his anxiety by putting distance between it and himself, instead of trying to avoid it."

The man had seemed determined at the beginning of the interview to deport Viktor and his family. In the end, he let Viktor go home, and Viktor thought his treatment using paradoxical intention must have been successful. He believed that the officer, instead of paying him a psychiatrist's fee, allowed him and his family to be spared temporarily, since neither the Gestapo nor the SS came to pick up the Frankl family.

Viktor and his family suffered many professional and personal indignities as Jews in Nazi Vienna. One that Viktor found especially painful was that the SS had outlawed mountain climbing for Jews. The Schneeberg and Rax mountains, among Viktor's favorites, had been off limits to him for a year, and he was yearning to climb, even dreaming of it at night. He had a non-Jewish friend, Hubert Gsur, who, unbeknownst to Viktor at the time, was living a dangerous double life. He was a member of the German army, the *Wehrmacht*, and at the same time an illegal Communist and member of the resistance against the Nazis.

Gsur knew how badly Viktor wanted, maybe even needed, to go mountain climbing. One day, wearing his Wehrmacht uniform to prevent suspicion, he came for Viktor and told him to cover the yellow star he was forced to wear. He took him to a mountain peak, the Hohe Wand. When they got there, Viktor was so overcome with emotion that he "kept on kissing the face of the rock in front of him." His hands delighted in its rough surface. With pleasure, he felt his unused muscles stretch and flex to obey his commands as he scaled the peak.

Later, Viktor was able to return the favor to Gsur, although in a very different way. The SS discovered Hubert Gsur's resistance work, and he was jailed and condemned to die. While Gsur was in prison, Viktor was laboriously pecking away on the typewriter, writing his first book, *The Doctor and the Soul*. Viktor hoped that if he wrote the book, even if he died in a concentration camp, the basic

information about logotherapy would be preserved for the world. At the time, the only way to make copies was by using dark-colored carbon paper and a second sheet of typing paper. Viktor did this so that Hubert's wife, Erna, could smuggle a copy into the jail, and Hubert could read the book while he sat on death row. After the war, people told Viktor that his book had given Hubert hope and courage to face his own death. Hubert was guillotined at the prison in 1944.

While Viktor treated patients and developed and wrote about logotherapy, he also made time for socializing, especially with women. Later in life, he said he had been promiscuous as a young medical student and resident. He had found it easy to get involved with many nurses without being serious about them. Every February, he also took advantage of *Fasching*, a season of carnival dances and balls, where alcohol flowed freely. At these events he picked out several young women he thought he would like to get involved with during the coming year.

If Viktor liked a woman and being straightforward didn't work, he tried to manipulate her into dating him. One young woman who

After the Nazi takeover of Austria, Viktor, as a Jew, was no longer permitted to climb his beloved Rax Mountain.

kept putting him off finally agreed to go with him to a lecture because he told her how fascinating the lecturer was. He did not tell her that he would be the speaker, but he hoped that she would be impressed enough to go out with him after he stepped onto the stage. He often used tricks like this to impress women and get what he wanted from them.

At the time, Viktor had already formed the logotherapy principle that sex should be an expression of love and that sexual partners should behave responsibly toward each other. He knew, as he pursued these young women for self-gratification, that he was violating his values, and while he went on dating widely, he felt remorse about not living up to his standards.

Viktor did develop serious relationships with three young women. The first was a woman named Lola, whom he met at a Socialist youth circle; she ended up marrying one of Viktor's colleagues. The second was someone with whom he struck up a conversation on a Vienna street, Rosl. With Rosl he had a short relationship, but it was deeply meaningful to him; she also married someone else.

When he was thirty-five, Viktor met the third young woman, Tilly Grosser, who was a nurse at the Rothschild Hospital. Right away, he noticed her curly black hair, her sparkling eyes, and her warm smile. Tilly was not especially attracted to Viktor, however. In fact, the opposite was true. She knew him as a man who had dated her best friend and then dropped her without explanation. She agreed to a date with Viktor because she wanted to get back at him for what he had done to her friend. Before she could do or say anything about what Viktor had done, he brought it up himself. His honesty impressed her, and she decided she would go out with him again.

It wasn't Tilly's beauty that caused Viktor to decide he wanted to marry her. He loved her intuitiveness and her understanding heart. Occasionally, she expressed herself in a naive way, and he found that refreshing. Then a rather simple, everyday experience tipped the scales and made Viktor feel he wanted to spend the rest of his life with Tilly.

Viktor and Tilly had been dating for a while when Tilly came to the Frankl apartment one day to prepare lunch for Viktor and his parents. It was nearly time to eat when the phone rang. Rothschild Hospital was calling with an emergency. A patient had attempted suicide with sleeping pills; because of the dire situation in Vienna, the Rothschild was receiving as many as ten patients a day who had tried suicide. Viktor had developed a neurosurgical technique that helped save the lives of people who had overdosed on medication. He injected a stimulant medication directly into one ventricle (one of four cavities in the brain that communicates with other ventricles and the central canal of the spinal cord) while draining the fourth ventricle. This was the fastest route by which the medication could stimulate vital activities like respiration. The hospital wanted Viktor to come and try his "brain-surgery magic" with the patient.

Viktor rushed out the door and hailed a taxicab, even

Viktor and Tilly's wedding portrait.

though it was illegal by then for Jews to use taxis. Two hours later, he returned home. His parents had eaten, but Tilly had waited for him. Instead of complaining that he had taken so long to get home, she showed genuine interest in what he had been doing. She asked how it had gone and whether he had been able to save the patient. That was the moment Viktor decided he wanted to marry Tilly Grosser.

There was a separate office in Nazi Vienna where Jews could obtain a marriage license, and the Nazis had announced that this office would close for good on December 31, 1941. Viktor and Tilly and Viktor's high school history teacher and his bride were the last four Jews in Vienna to receive marriage licenses during the war. After getting the license, Viktor and Tilly became Viktor and Tilly Frankl under a *chuppe*, the traditional Jewish wedding canopy, at the Jewish Community Center. Afterward, they walked home, Tilly in a dark dress and pillbox hat with a full-face veil and Viktor in a pinstripe suit. Both of them wore the yellow Jewish star on their wedding best, and they walked because they were forbidden the use of streetcars and taxis. Tilly moved in with Viktor and his parents, into his childhood home on Czerningasse, because no new housing was available to Jews.

FoUR

Say Yes to Life
In Spite of Everything

At first glance, Sperlgymnasium, Viktor Frankl's high school, looks like just one more apartment building on Kleine Sperlgasse. Its light gray façade is flush with the fronts of the apartments attached to it on either side. On a late September day in 1942, however, it stood out from the other buildings because lines of people, old and young, crowded through its front doors. They carried suitcases, hatboxes, and bundles—anything that would hold the ten kilos of baggage they had been told to bring with them.

Sperlgymnasium, once a familiar part of Viktor's everyday life, had been transformed into a place of humiliation and fear. The day before, he and Tilly and their parents had received the long-dreaded phone call ordering them to report to the high school. As Viktor and his father walked up the steps, memories of friends and teachers, lessons and games must have flooded through them. They could easily visualize their past in the school corridors and classrooms; their future, on the other hand, was a total unknown.

The Nazis had turned Sperlgymnasium into a processing center. Viktor was taken to a room where he had his head shaved. When he came out, he didn't recognize the frail, beardless, bald man who stood in front of him. He was stunned to realize that he was looking at his father. The dignified old man, who had had a full head of white hair and had worn a beautifully trimmed beard and mustache, had disappeared. Viktor was filled with pity for his father and said later, "It was such a degrading thing, as though he were a murderer on his way to prison." By silent agreement, Viktor and his father never talked to each other about this humiliating experience.

Jewish families waiting to be deported.

With all the uncertainty and changes facing the captives, it isn't surprising that Viktor couldn't remember years later whether he and his family had slept in the high school for one night or two. On September 24, the Frankl family and thirteen hundred other Jews were shoved into waiting trucks and driven to the Aspang Station for deportation. At the station, most of the prisoners were pushed into crowded freight cars. A group of Jewish psychiatric patients were part of the transport, and one of the doctors from the Rothschild had recommended to the Gestapo that Viktor be sent with them to help keep them calm. These patients rode in a single old passenger car, and because Viktor supervised their care, he and his family didn't have to ride in the freight cars, which were so crowded that people had to take turns squatting on the floor and standing.

The transport ended at Bauschowitz, a small town in northern Czechoslovakia. The prisoners walked for an hour, carrying their luggage, to reach the Theresienstadt camp. Before November 1941, Theresienstadt had been a fortress town with about four thousand residents. By the time the Frankls arrived less than a year later, fifty-three thousand Jews were living in the same amount of space. From here, people were transported to ghettos, places where Jews were forced to live apart from the rest of the population, and where they were often immediately killed; or they were sent to extermination camps, such as Auschwitz. Although Theresienstadt was considered less dangerous than many other camps and has also been referred to at times as a ghetto, during its four-year history as a camp, thirty-three thousand people died there of starvation and disease. The year the Frankl family arrived, a crematorium was built in Theresienstadt for the incineration of nearly two hundred bodies a day.

In their continuing attempts to keep the extermination camps a secret, the Nazis used several methods to hide what they were doing. Choosing isolated sites, such as Auschwitz, was one of them. At different times, they discussed confining Jews to ghettos until Germany won the war, making it easier to then exterminate them, because world opinion would have become unimportant. As it was, the rest of the world did very little to interfere with the Final Solution, even when governments became aware of it.

An exception was the Danish Red Cross, which insisted on inspecting the quarters at Theresienstadt, where Danish Jews were confined. In 1944, the Nazis used Theresienstadt to fool the inspection team into thinking the concentration camps were simply ghettos. Before the Red Cross came, the Nazis transported a large number of Theresienstadt inmates to other camps and ghettos, so that Theresienstadt would not appear overcrowded. The prisoners who stayed at Theresienstadt participated in "beautifying" the camp—planting gardens and painting houses. The Nazis also made a propaganda film following the "beautification," portraying Theresienstadt as a place where Jews were happy, well fed, and well dressed. The film was called *Der Führer schenkt den Juden eine Stadt* (*The Führer Gives the Jews a City*). When the inspection team left, the deportation of prisoners to extermination camps continued. However, because the Danish Red Cross had been so persistent, the Danish Jews were given better quarters than other prisoners, and none of them were transported from Theresienstadt to the death camps.

Many of the people interned at Theresienstadt were famous—Jewish leaders, doctors, lawyers, artists, and musicians. When the Red Cross visited, the inmates presented cultural events for the inspectors. But even when the Red Cross wasn't there, the prisoners tried to keep their lives stimulating and meaningful. Viktor participated by offering a lecture series that included such topics as "The Psychology of Alpinism [mountain climbing]" and "How Can I Keep My Nerves Healthy?" As he had done for young people in Vienna, he organized suicide-prevention teams that helped people adjust to life at Theresienstadt.

Daily life in the camp was a strange combination of exquisite beauty and extreme pain and torture. On the one hand, artists and children painted, actors performed plays, symphony orchestras played the music of the great composers, and scholars like Viktor conducted lectures. On the other hand, at the eastern edge of the camp stood the Little Fortress, a police prison. The Gestapo ran the prison for the purpose of controlling, torturing, and often

killing Theresienstadt inmates and others the Nazis wanted to punish.

One day, for no reason Viktor could ever figure out, an SS officer sent him to the Little Fortress. Although rain was pelting down, an officer told him to fill a bucket with water, run to a compost pile, and pour the water over the top of it. The garbage heap was taller than Viktor, so he couldn't reach the top. When he splashed water on the sides of the pile, the officer punched him. For hours he ran back and forth in the rain. Each time he missed the top of the heap, he was beaten. At last he was dragged back to his barracks.

At first Tilly was shocked when she saw Viktor. Then the nurse in her took charge, and she cleaned and bandaged his wounds. To take his mind off what had happened, she took him to a jazz concert in one of the barracks. Later Viktor wrote, "The contrast between

Theresienstadt was a transit camp for prominent Jewish artists and intellectuals and their families. As this photo of a teenage girl shows, people wore their own clothes and could move about the camp on their own. Nevertheless, the death rate reached 200 per day, and the anxiety on this girl's face is clear.

the indescribable tortures of the morning and the jazz in the evening was typical of our existence—with all its contradictions of beauty and hideousness, humanity and inhumanity."

Viktor's father was so weak that when the family had walked from the Bauschowitz station to the camp, he could only carry a hatbox with a few belongings in it. Food was so scarce that one day someone saw Gabriel Frankl picking potato peelings from a trashcan. After six months at Theresienstadt, Mr. Frankl died of starvation and pneumonia at the age of eighty-one. Viktor felt at peace because he knew he had done all he could for his father by staying in Vienna and being with him until a few hours before his death.

Although people died every day in Theresienstadt, the prisoners constantly feared being sent to a worse camp. When they were called up, many people tried to believe the guards who told them they were being deported to a better ghetto. As the war continued, however, they knew from reports by prisoners who had escaped the annihilation camps that deportation almost certainly meant death.

The prison courtyard of the Little Fortress at Theresienstadt, used by the Gestapo to torture prisoners, in a photograph taken after the war. It was here that Viktor was beaten and made to run in the rain while he watered a compost pile.

In May 1944, when she was only forty-nine years old, Tilly's mother was transported to Auschwitz and killed. A few months later, in October 1944, Viktor was called up for deportation. Tilly was not on the deportation list because she was working as a slave laborer in a factory that made ammunition for the German army. The factory people told her she would not be deported for two years because of her "job." Now she wanted to go with Viktor. They sat together and talked about what to do. Viktor begged her not to volunteer for the transport. He was afraid that the Nazis would think she was trying to get out of helping with the war effort and that if she volunteered, they might punish her severely. He also thought that if she stayed in Theresienstadt, she might have a better chance of surviving. But Tilly was determined. She requested and was granted permission to leave on the same transport as Viktor.

Viktor was surprised that his mother, Elsa, wasn't on the deportation list. She was sixty-five years old, and older people were usually among the first to go. He began to hope that she could stay at Theresienstadt, where she could possibly survive. When the day of the transport dawned, Viktor made his way to where his mother stood. He told her goodbye. Then suddenly, at the last minute, he asked, "Please give me your blessing."

His mother cried, "Yes! Yes, I bless you!" Later Viktor wrote, "I can never forget how she cried out, from deep within her heart."

Viktor and Tilly boarded the train, and uncertainty bore down on them with all its heaviness. Would Viktor ever see his mother again? Where were they headed? The prisoners wishfully told themselves they might be leaving for slave labor in a munitions factory. Two hundred fifty miles later, the train slowed, and voices cried out, "There is a sign, 'Auschwitz'!" The name *Auschwitz* "stood for all that was horrible: gas chambers, crematoriums, massacres." As dawn light came, the prisoners saw before them a huge camp.

Electricrified barbed wire was strung between hook-shaped concrete posts. Shots rang out from the two-story watchtowers. Viktor saw rows and rows of prisoners wearing nothing but rags.

Viktor and Tilly left the train and stood together, waiting for the first selection to take place. Selections would become a daily part of their existence, the means of separating those who would live from those who would die. The first separation was women from men. Before that happened, Viktor had some parting words for Tilly. He told her, "Tilly, stay alive at any price. Do you hear? At any price." He meant that if a situation ever arose in which her life could be saved by giving herself sexually to the guards, her life was of far more value than being faithful to him. She indicated that she understood. Viktor believed that since Tilly was fifteen years younger than he was, she had a better chance of surviving than he did. His last words before their separation were intended to increase her chances.

Tilly was sent with the women prisoners, and Viktor found himself standing before a man who, with the casual flick of a gloved finger, determined the fate of human lives. If he pointed left, it meant immediate death. A finger to the right was for those who could provide the Nazis with slave labor. Years later, Viktor wondered if the man was Dr. Josef Mengele, who was notorious in Auschwitz for his cool, gloved decision-making and for the terrible experiments he conducted on prisoners. Mengele's name still strikes terror in the hearts of survivors today. When Viktor went forward, the man with the gloves pointed left. Viktor didn't know anyone in the left line, so behind the officer's back, he switched to the right side, where he saw some doctors he knew. Later he said, "Only God knows where I got that idea or found the courage." This was only the first of many times when Viktor's life would be saved by a snap decision or some small incident that seemed to happen by chance.

Hoarse shouts ordered Viktor and his fellow prisoners to run from the selection station to the cleansing station. When they reached the shed, SS men told them to toss their valuables onto blankets spread on the ground. Viktor and Tilly had already thrown away their wedding rings to keep the Nazis from getting them. But Viktor had hidden his two prize possessions in his coat. The first was the manuscript of his book about logotherapy, the one he hoped would be his legacy if he died. The other reminded him of the thrilling hours he had spent scaling the soaring Austrian mountain peaks—the Donauland Alpine Club pin he had earned as a climbing guide. Since he had no valuables to throw onto the blankets, Viktor hoped he would be able to keep his coat with its precious contents.

However, the men were herded to a room just outside the showers, and an SS man barked that they had two minutes to leave their clothes in a pile and carry their shoes with them. Into the pile went Viktor's coat, his lifework, and the reminder of his time on the mountains. With the other prisoners, he ran to another room.

A sign on barbed wire at Auschwitz warns, "Danger! High Voltage!"

Having his head shaved at Sperlgymnasium had humiliated him two years earlier, but now all the hair on his body was shaved off. Mercilessly, the guards kept the men moving, this time to the showers. Shocks of fear jolted through the prisoners. They had heard stories about prisoners being told to get ready for showers, even given bars of soap, only to realize as the door clanged shut that gas, not water, was entering the chamber. Relief washed over Viktor and the other inmates as real water poured from the showerheads.

When Viktor emerged from the showers, all he had left were his body, his glasses, his shoes, and a belt he would later trade for a piece of bread. Outside the showers lay huge piles of ragged clothing. The former owners of the clothes no longer needed them; they had been gassed. The prisoners were now ordered to find something, anything, to wear from the piles. Bereft of the book that was like his child, Viktor took a thin, torn coat from the heap. As he slipped his hand into one of the pockets, he felt the crinkle of a scrap of paper. He pulled it out and looked at it. It was a torn page from a Jewish prayer book. On it was written the Shema Yisrael, the prayer Viktor had seen and heard his father say every day when he was a boy: "Hear, O Israel, the Lord our God, the Lord is One God; and you shall love the Lord your God with all your heart and with all your soul and with all your strength." Viktor later wrote that finding this prayer in his "new" coat was a "challenge to me *to live* what I had written, to practice what I had preached." He kept that scrap of paper with him until he was liberated.

Auschwitz was actually made up of three huge camps, known as Auschwitz I, II, and III, and forty smaller subcamps. Auschwitz II was also called Birkenau, and it was the largest of the three camps. Row upon row of wooden and brick barracks were lined up as precisely as the white markers of a military cemetery. Three hundred buildings housed as many as ninety thousand prisoners at any given time. The inmates slept three to a wooden bunk and had to share a single thin blanket. The SS guards constantly checked on the prisoners and beat them for no reason. It was in Birkenau that more than a million Jews were gassed and cremated. And it was in one of the barracks of Birkenau that Viktor found himself now, still alive, reeling from the shock of all that had happened during the selections.

That first evening, Viktor looked around for a friend who had also been on his transport. He couldn't find him, so he asked a prisoner who had been at Auschwitz for a while if he could tell him anything.

"Was he sent to the left side?" the man asked.

A 1944 aerial reconnaissance photo showing U.S. bombs (in the upper left) falling on the crematoria of Auschwitz II Camp (Birkenau). The photo gives some indication of the enormous size of the camp.

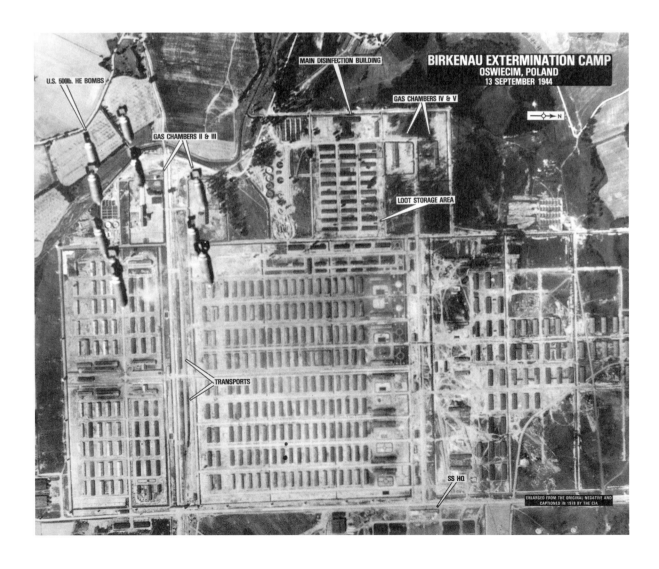

"Yes."

"Then," the man said with cruel humor, "you can see him there."

Viktor was confused. "Where?"

The man pointed to the tall chimney several hundred yards from where they stood. Red flames and oily black smoke belched into the gray skies of Poland. "That's where your friend is, floating up to Heaven."

Still Viktor did not understand, perhaps because what the man was telling him was too hard to believe. After all, he had just seen his friend earlier that day, and for a few moments, he himself had stood on the left side. Finally, someone explained in plain words that his friend had been gassed and cremated. At last Viktor grasped the awful truth: among the thousands of burning bodies was the body of his friend.

On his second night in Auschwitz-Birkenau, exhausted from all he had gone through, Viktor was awakened from a deep sleep by wild party music. A camp warden was holding a celebration. Suddenly, the music stopped. A few moments later, a violin began playing an exquisitely sad melody. It was October 23, 1944, the night of Tilly's twenty-fourth birthday, and as Viktor listened, he grieved over their separation. He hadn't seen her since they stood on the platform beside the train. She could be a few hundred feet away, separated from him by barbed wire; she could be miles away; she could already have been gassed. He had no way of knowing.

After only three or four days at Auschwitz-Birkenau, Viktor and a group of other prisoners were loaded onto a freight train. They had no idea where they were going, and their lives depended on the direction the train took. Anxiously, they tried to guess its destination. As it moved westward, they thought they might be headed for Mauthausen, a camp that was so well known for torture that even Auschwitz prisoners feared being sent there. When the train

swerved away from Mauthausen onto a bridge that led to Dachau in southern Germany, the prisoners danced for joy. Later, Frankl would point out that "the 'size' of human suffering is absolutely relative" and that "a very trifling thing can cause the greatest of joys." In itself, going to Dachau was far from cause for elation, but compared with being sent to Mauthausen and an almost certain agonizing death, it was something to celebrate. When the men reached Dachau, they were sent to one of its subcamps, Kaufering III. They felt gratitude once again: prisoners who had been there for a while told them there were no ovens, no gas chambers, and no crematoria.

Kaufering III was surrounded by Bavarian forests. Through a frame of barbed wire, the prisoners could see flowering green hills backed by dark blue mountains. How different that view was from the miserable gray mud huts with underground wooden sleeping shelves into which the prisoners crowded each night.

The chimney of the crematorium looms large in this photograph of Dachau Concentration Camp, taken after liberation. The soldiers in front of the building are American; the bodies to the left are German guards they had shot.

Inmates on the sleeping shelves inside a dugout, A-frame barrack at Kaufering. Viktor stayed in a hut like this at both Kaufering and Türkheim.

Because he was a doctor, Viktor might have been assigned to care for patients in the camp infirmary, or he might have received some other kind of lighter work. But after his release, he said he was proud that he had been able to survive as a manual laborer during most of his time in the camps. With very little food, thin rags for clothing, and shoes that barely fit because his feet were swollen, he worked on railroads, dug ditches, and helped to construct a new camp. What he had learned as a mountain climber helped him endure the heavy work. Once a fellow prisoner, watching him move a wagon loaded with sick prisoners, observed, "Frankl, I see from how you are proceeding that you have a way of conserving your energy when you are not using it to do something, like an Alpine climbing guide."

In order to survive, the prisoners focused their dreams, fantasies, and energy on the smallest details of getting food, getting a better piece of clothing, avoiding punishment. Yet one day, Viktor realized that it was not the minutiae of day-to-day existence that enabled him to go on. Rather, looking to the future and thinking about his goals pulled him through. He had this realization while he was caught up in what he called "the endless little problems of our miserable life"—whether there would be sausage in the evening's rations, whether to exchange it for a piece of bread, how to get a piece of wire to tie his shoes, how to get a Capo (a prisoner with extra privileges who acted as a foreman) to give him a safer job.

Suddenly, Viktor felt disgusted by his preoccupations. He began to daydream instead about standing on the platform of a warm, well-lit lecture hall. He saw himself lecturing about the psychology of the concentration camps. This dream became his goal, and ironically, focusing on that dream, rather than on survival, is what helped him survive. He wrote, "I succeeded somehow in rising above the situation, above the sufferings of the moment."

As time passed, Viktor noticed that often the physically strong men were not the ones who survived. He concluded that survival depended more on people's inner strength, on their ability to use this horrible experience to grow as individuals. One day, as he dug a trench under gray skies, surrounded by gray snow, he struggled inside himself to try to find a reason for his suffering. He found himself asking whether there was any purpose to life. He struggled with the answer, and from deep inside himself he "heard a victorious 'Yes.'" Just then, he looked up, and a light went on in a farmhouse on the horizon. Later he would write, "and the light shineth in the darkness," regarding the pinprick of light that had coincided with his deep inner "Yes."

There was a strict rule in the camps against trying to save a man in the process of committing suicide, and suicide was common. Yet many times, Viktor spoke to someone who was considering killing himself. His approach was always to try to help the person find something to live for, something that only that person could do or be—whether it was to be a father to his child now in hiding or to complete some scientific research he had begun.

Occasionally, Viktor was given the opportunity to talk to a whole group of men, to try to give them hope in what seemed like a hopeless situation. Once, a prisoner broke into the camp storehouse and stole some potatoes. The authorities said that if the other prisoners didn't identify the perpetrator, they would all starve for a day. Even though the inmates were already starving, they chose not to eat rather than send their fellow prisoner to certain death. They sat in their barracks that evening with flattened stomachs, shivering and deeply discouraged.

The barracks warden, also a prisoner, asked Viktor to speak some words of encouragement to the men. Viktor was exhausted and feeling very low himself, but he felt he could not pass up this opportunity to serve his comrades. He talked to them for about an hour, and they listened without a sound. He spoke about the future, about loved ones or a special task that might be waiting for them. He talked about many ways of finding meaning in their situation. He said that there could even be meaning in choosing to meet their suffering or their dying with courage and dignity. He quoted the philosopher Friedrich Nietzsche: "That which does not kill me makes me stronger." When Viktor was finished talking, the men walked over to thank him with tears in their eyes.

In March 1945, after performing five months of hard labor at Kaufering, Viktor was asked whether he wanted to join a transport headed for a so-called rest camp, Türkheim, where he would work as a doctor. Transports constantly moved prisoners in and out of camps all over Europe. Sometimes prisoners were asked to volunteer for a transport. The officials would tell them where it was going and what kinds of rewards there might be for the work they would be required to do. But the men never knew for sure if the transport was really going where the authorities said it was. Viktor's friends were afraid that the offer was a trick and begged him not to go. At this point, Viktor looked like a walking skeleton and felt that he would probably die in a very short time. He decided that if he spent his last remaining weeks or months caring for sick prisoners, at least his death would have some meaning. He agreed to go.

There was one thing he felt he must do before he left. He still believed that Tilly's youth made her chances for survival greater than his, especially now, as he felt he was close to death. He wanted to make a will, although he had no possessions to leave to her. He turned to a friend, a man named Otto, and made him memorize the words he wanted Tilly to hear. He asked Otto to tell her three things: that he had thought of her every hour, every day; that he had loved her more than he had ever loved anyone; and that the short time they were married had outweighed everything, "even all we have gone through here."

When he got to Türkheim, Viktor found that it didn't look very different from Kaufering. The prisoners' shelters at both places were huts with A-shaped roofs aboveground and walls dug into the earth. Viktor had helped build these huts while he was at Kaufering, which was not far away. There was not much he could do as a doctor in the camp. Most of his patients suffered from typhus, a disease carried by lice. Infected prisoners got high fevers with delirium. The hallucinations came upon them when they slept, and it was then that most of them died. When he had a few aspirin, he would give them to the patients who were very sick but still had a chance to survive. He sat with the others and tried to offer them comfort. When Viktor himself contracted typhus, he kept himself from delirium and death by forcing himself to stay awake at night. A friend smuggled him scraps of official Nazi papers, and on the backs of these, he began to

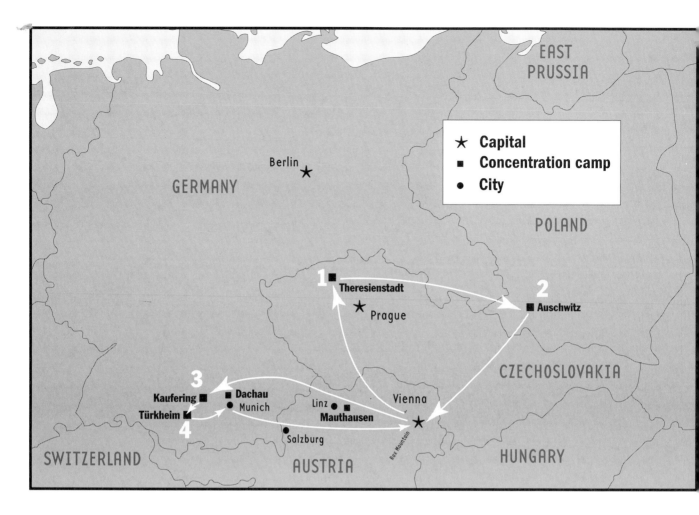

Viktor Frankl's movements from the time of deportation from Vienna in 1942 to his return after liberation in 1945.

rewrite the book he had lost at Auschwitz, *The Doctor and the Soul.* Writing kept him awake, and staying awake helped keep him alive.

As the battlefront came closer and closer to Türkheim in the spring of 1945, the prisoners could hear cannons and gunfire. All over Europe, the British, Russians, and Americans were closing in on the German army. Resistance groups from the occupied countries joined the fight. With sounds of the war nearing them, the prisoners' hopes rose and fell.

Within the camp, changes seemed to occur by the minute. In many camps, as the liberating armies drew near, the SS forced inmates to evacuate and march, often to their deaths. The officers were trying to do away with evidence that could later incriminate

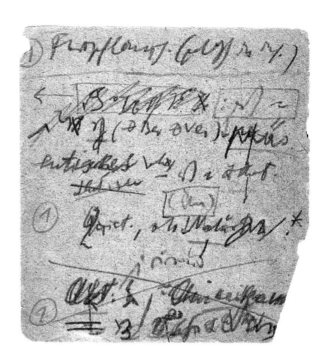

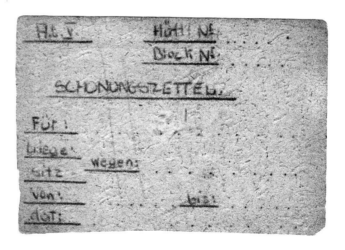

Scraps of camp forms on which Viktor rewrote The Doctor and the Soul.

Earthen barracks at Kaufering, photographed after liberation. It is possible that those are prisoners' bodies lying in the road.

them. Guards told the Türkheim prisoners they would have to leave so the camp could be burned. When transport trucks did not arrive, Viktor and a friend, fearing they would be burned alive, planned an escape. While Viktor waited for the man to get some bread, an International Red Cross vehicle rolled into camp. Viktor was astonished and thrilled that he would not have to risk running.

Red Cross representatives told the prisoners not to leave the camp, that an agreement protecting them had already been signed. Then the team left to set up headquarters at a nearby farmhouse. That night the SS guards piled the inmates into trucks. They told the men they were lucky, because they were to be exchanged for Swiss prisoners of war. Viktor and his companion were disappointed and angry when the chief doctor told them there wasn't room for them on the trucks. Weeks later, they learned that those prisoners had been taken to another camp, locked into huts, and burned to death.

Viktor and his friend, exhausted by the alternating hope and disillusionment of the past few days, fell asleep. Brilliant flashes of light and the roar of cannons awakened them during the night. The battlefront had finally reached them. Quickly, they rolled from the wooden sleeping shelves onto the floor for safety. By morning the shooting had slowed, and a white flag flew above the camp. It was April 27, 1945, and victorious American troops from Texas entered to set them free.

At last Viktor and the other prisoners who were still in camp could taste liberty, but by this time, they had become so numb to any emotions, that at first, they were hardly able to feel happiness at their newfound freedom. Viktor described walking out of the camp with his fellow prisoners into a meadow filled with flowers. He wrote, "We had no feelings about them. The first spark of joy came when we saw a rooster with a tail of multicolored feathers. But it remained only a spark; we did not yet belong to this world."

Young survivors behind barbed wire, after liberation.

A medical report on Viktor's condition at the time of liberation showed that he had gained weight since he had left Kaufering III—enough to weigh a whole eighty-three pounds! The report showed that he "had irregular heart rhythms and quite probably a damaged heart muscle, edema from hunger, and frostbite on three fingers." Despite his poor physical condition, Viktor Frankl had survived more than two and a half years in not one but four concentration camps. The spirit of his survival is expressed in the title of a book he wrote later: . . . *trotzdem Ja zum Leben sagen (Say Yes to Life in Spite of Everything).*

FIVe

FINDING MEANING IN TRAGEDY

A few days after his liberation, Viktor again walked through meadows near the camp, and the ability to experience enjoyment and gratitude began to return to him. He watched larks soar above him and heard them sing. He saw and felt the expansiveness of the open fields and sky around him. He fell to his knees among the flowers. Over and over again, he found himself saying, "I called to the Lord from my narrow prison and He answered me in the freedom of space."

Viktor knew nothing about what had happened to Tilly, his mother, or his brother and sister-in-law. He wanted to return to Vienna, but the border between Germany and Austria was closed. He worked for two months in a hospital near Türkheim for displaced persons (people who had been removed to places far from home and had no way to get back after the war). He then headed for Munich, Germany, which brought him a little closer to Vienna. There he continued to work on the book he had lost. He also gave talks on Radio Munich about psychological problems people might face during the reconstruction of Europe.

One day when Viktor was walking in a field outside Munich, he came across a displaced person from Holland. The two men stopped to talk, and Viktor noticed that the man was holding and playing with something. "What do you have there?" he asked. The Dutch man showed him a small golden globe with blue enamel oceans. On the gold band representing the equator were engraved the words, "The whole world turns on love."

Viktor must have felt a multitude of emotions when he saw that pendant. It was exactly like one he had bought for Tilly as a birthday present. In fact, it might have been the same one, because the jeweler who sold it to him had said there was only one other one like it in Vienna. It was one of the treasures Tilly had given up at Auschwitz. He knew there was a nearby storehouse of jewelry from the concentration camps and thought perhaps the Dutchman had somehow gotten it from there. Without asking how the man had come by it, Viktor bought the pendant. He noticed that it had a small dent in it, but, he said, "The whole world still turned on love." Since he, now forty years old, had survived, he thought it was even more likely that Tilly, at twenty-five, was still alive, and he imagined giving her the pendant, possibly for the second time, when he saw her again.

Although he now possessed the necklace that might have been Tilly's, Viktor still knew nothing about his family. He was sure he would be able to learn more in Austria, and in August 1945, four months after his liberation, he prepared to leave for Vienna, the city he called home. In his pack, he put five things: a necktie he had rescued from storage at Türkheim after scraping lice eggs from it; letters of reference from the radio station in Munich; the torn page from the Jewish prayer book he had found at Auschwitz; the blue and gold pendant; and, most important, the scraps of paper on which he had begun to rewrite *The Doctor and the Soul.* On his last day in Munich, he received the painful news that his mother had been gassed as soon as she had arrived at Auschwitz-Birkenau. She had been sent there four days after Viktor and Tilly were deported from Theresienstadt, so it is possible that Viktor was still there when she entered the camp.

When Viktor arrived in Vienna, the city was scarcely recognizable as his home. For the last two years of the war, the Allied forces had bombed Vienna intensely in their fight against the Germans. In April 1945, the Soviet Union had attacked the city with heavy artillery. Fighting in the center of the city had been fierce, and Vienna had fallen to the Red Army on April 13, 1945. Nearly all the once-majestic public buildings on the Ringstrasse were badly damaged. Eighty-six thousand homes had been reduced to ruins. Houses and apartments that were still standing had empty sockets for windows.

After making broadcasts in Munich, Viktor continued to participate in radio programs when he returned to Vienna. Here he is, around 1947, in discussion with Father Diego Goetz, Heinz von Foerster, and a woman identified only as Ms. Bauer.

Everywhere he looked, Viktor saw piles of rubble the size of small mountains. The outside walls of St. Stephan's Cathedral, where Viktor had gone to think about whether to care for his parents or escape the Nazis by emigrating to the United States, were black from fire. The Prater, where he had spent so many happy days as a child and teenager, was reduced to weeds and rubble, except for the huge Ferris wheel, which had been hit in a bombing raid but was still standing.

Something else had changed dramatically: the 170,000 Jews who had formed a thriving community in Vienna had all but disappeared, along with their schools, synagogues, and libraries. Almost as if in their place, American, Russian, British, and French soldiers, who formed the postwar government and police power of Vienna, filled the streets.

With the city in ruins and most of his community gone, Viktor needed to find a place to stay. He spent his first night in the Jewish nursing home where he had sent patients to save them before he was deported. The following morning, an employee of the nursing home gave Viktor the crushing news that Tilly was dead. He learned that after he had last seen her at Auschwitz, she had been sent to the Bergen-Belsen camp. When British soldiers liberated the camp, they found close to seventeen thousand unburied corpses. Approximately seventeen thousand more of the sixty thousand prisoners still living died of starvation, exhaustion, and disease before they could be treated. Tilly was one of them.

After hearing the news about Tilly, Viktor rented some rooms in a basement, where he stayed for two weeks. As the days went by, he learned that his brother and sister-in-law had most likely died while working as slave laborers in a mine that was part of an Auschwitz subcamp. He would never know for certain what had happened to them.

Sitting alone in his basement rooms, Viktor began to feel after all he had survived that his life wasn't worth living. The hope of reuniting with Tilly and his mother had given him something to live for while he dug ditches and suffered beatings. Now when he visited his friends, he broke down and sobbed. He was so deeply depressed that they were afraid he might commit suicide. But even as he did think of killing himself, Viktor kept feeling that life was asking something from him, that his life must still have a purpose. He told one friend, "When all this happens to someone, to be tested in such a way, . . . it must have some meaning. I have a feeling . . . that I am destined for something."

Viktor's friends, mostly fellow physicians and colleagues from before the war, supported him in every way they could as he tried to rebuild his life. One man in particular, Dr. Bruno Pitterman, helped him get settled. He gave him an old typewriter, so he could work on *The Doctor and the Soul*. He also found an apartment building where Viktor could serve as the manager. In exchange, Viktor got a single corner room in a flat he shared with other people who had lost their homes during the war. None of the people knew each other. Viktor's room had cardboard for windows, a narrow bed, a small stove, a cabinet, and a table where he put the old typewriter.

As Viktor tried to adjust to living in a Vienna that no longer seemed like home, he encountered non-Jews who had been able to stay in the city throughout the war. Many of them suggested that his concentration camp experiences were no worse than what they had gone through. They said things like "We, too, have suffered." They also claimed that they knew nothing about the camps. These responses made the return to a normal life more difficult for Viktor and his fellow prisoners; survivors naturally felt deeply disappointed and bitter when the people they came back to denied the horror of their experience.

In the camps, Viktor had kept his eyes on the future to give him hope. His first hope had been to see his family again, to start a new life with them. The other had been to continue his work and to make use of what he had learned in the camps in that work. Now he had lost half of his reason for living.

In his grief, he turned to his work. He began to look through the scraps of paper he had scribbled on while at Türkheim. He got ahold of the copy of the original manuscript of *The Doctor and the Soul,* which he had left in Vienna with a friend when he was deported. Using these, he rewrote the book, and this helped him cope with the deaths of his family members. He was still considering suicide but decided he would at least wait until the book was finished. "Beyond that," he said, "I didn't want to exist." Finding a purpose, even though he felt it was temporary, helped him live through those first few weeks without his family.

While he was still at Türkheim, Viktor had written a chapter on the psychology of the camps. He added it to the end of *The Doctor and the Soul.* Viktor was thrilled when at last he took the book to the publisher. He wrote, "As I look back, the most rewarding hour for

Vienna, 1946. The city still lay in ruins, even months after Viktor's return.

me was delivering the final version . . . to my very first publisher." He was also relieved, because at last the book that had seen so many near deaths was coming to life.

Very soon after he took *The Doctor and the Soul* to the publisher, Viktor decided he needed to write another book. Perhaps he was motivated in part by the satisfying feeling of accomplishment. Also, as he wrote the chapter about his camp experiences, powerful memories were stirred. He now felt he must write a book devoted just to those ordeals. Friends who had read the chapter about the camps in his first book agreed and encouraged him to write more. In the space of nine days, he dictated the entire manuscript of the account of his time in the concentration camps. Viktor paced up and down in his chilly, unheated room, speaking almost nonstop. When he did stop, it was often to break down crying as he relived his incredibly painful experiences.

Viktor was determined to publish the book anonymously. He believed this was the only way he could tell such vivid, personal stories from his heart. He also felt strongly that he did not want the book to bring him personal recognition. His friends, however, saw it differently. They said that putting his name on the book was a matter of accepting responsibility for what he had written, and they began pressuring him. At the last minute, as he later wrote, "I saw that as an anonymous publication it would lose half its value, and that I must have the courage to state my convictions openly." The first edition went to press with his name only on the title page, not on the cover. The book was called *Ein Psycholog erlebt das Konzentrationslager (A Psychologist Experiences the Concentration Camp)* and is titled *Man's Search for Meaning* in English.

Ironically, although Viktor had not wanted to call attention to himself through the publication of *Man's Search for Meaning*, it made him more famous than any of the other thirty-one books he wrote. Many Holocaust survivors have written books and articles about their experiences, but Viktor Frankl's, first published in Austria in 1946, was one of the earliest. It has been read in high school and university classes across the United States, and by 1984, five American colleges had chosen it as the book of the year. In 1991, a joint project by the Library of Congress and the Book of the Month Club named *Man's Search for Meaning* one of the ten most influential books in America.

Viktor's account of the Holocaust was substantially different from most others. Even though he told a very personal story, he

The cover of the first edition of Man's Search for Meaning.

also stepped back from the situation and analyzed it as a psychiatrist. A major focus of his analysis is the observation that concentration camp prisoners went through three main psychological stages during their incarceration.

The first stage was the phase of *adjustment* to unbelievably awful circumstances. Initially, prisoners felt only shock and disbelief about what was happening to them and the people around them. Often people's first defense against an overwhelming experience is denial. Prisoners tell themselves that this can't really be happening, or, as Viktor put it, they have a "delusion of reprieve"; in other words, they believe that something or someone will still save them from the situation.

After the initial shock, prisoners began to adjust to camp life. They developed a kind of "cold curiosity" about what was going to happen next. They wondered, almost as if they were scientists, how camp life was going to affect them. Frankl said that this objectivity was a way of defending themselves from feeling too deeply about was happening. To their surprise, prisoners learned that the things they had been taught all their lives were not necessarily true. For example, they couldn't brush their teeth, and their diet should have caused gum disease, but their gums stayed healthy. In Viktor's words, the prisoners discovered that "man can get used to anything, but do not ask us how." The shock and denial of the first stage were over within a few days.

Frankl observed that the second stage of concentration camp life was characterized by *apathy*. He called it "a kind of emotional death" and explained how apathy was necessary for survival. For example, new prisoners were assigned to clean the sewage from the latrines and carry it out to the fields. If the prisoners showed that they were disgusted, the Capos beat them. Not caring, or at the very least, not showing that they cared, lessened their torture.

Viktor described a poignant example of apathy. He wrote about a prisoner (possibly himself) watching while a doctor picked the black, gangrenous toes off the feet of a twelve-year-old boy one by one. He wrote that the onlooker "stood unmoved." Apathy had both a cause and an effect. It could be caused by any number of camp conditions: lack of food, loss of sleep due to the infestation of lice, the knowledge that torture would follow if a person showed feelings, the inability to predict what might happen next, and loss of self-esteem. The effect of apathy was that it helped the prisoners survive, and survival was the main focus of the second stage.

The third stage of concentration camp life was *liberation and recovery*. Viktor compared this stage to the experience of a deep-sea diver returning to the surface. If a diver returns too quickly, pressure decreases too quickly, resulting in severe pains and possibly even death. In the same way, prisoners could have a severe reaction to being suddenly freed, to having the pressure relieved too quickly. Recovery and a return to normal life needed to proceed gradually.

The apathy that had helped the prisoners survive in stage two did not just go away with liberation. Released captives often felt as if they were in a dream. Just as they had emotionally distanced themselves from the horrors of concentration camp life, they continued to distance themselves from their newfound freedom. Frankl identified this behavior as *depersonalization*. He wrote about how, throughout the war, the prisoners had dreamed of returning to their families, their homes, their work. Now, when their dreams had the possibility of reality, everything seemed unreal, as if it were happening to someone else. They were depersonalizing their freedom.

After their release, the natural response for many prisoners was to long for revenge. Viktor believed that the desire for revenge required healing; he did not believe it should be encouraged. He wrote about a man who had been a good companion in camp and continued to be afterward. Nevertheless, voicing the feelings of many, this man said, "May [my] hand be cut off if I don't stain it with blood on the day when I get home!" Viktor wrote, "Only slowly could these men be guided back to the commonplace truth that no one has the right to do wrong, not even if wrong has been done to them." The bitterness

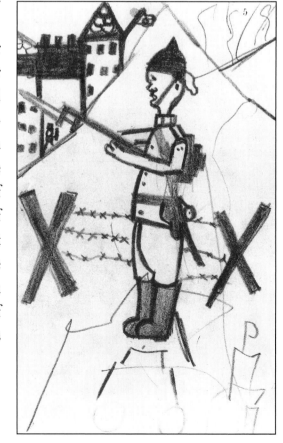

A drawing by a young Jewish boy whose family escaped to Shanghai, China, in 1939. He had lived through Kristallnacht, and his father went into hiding to avoid deportation. The child's drawing gives some indication of the deep impact of his experiences, even though he was not sent to a concentration camp.

and disillusionment felt by the released prisoners often increased when they found, as Viktor had, that their homes were no longer there, that the dreams that had kept them alive could never be realized, that their former neighbors and friends did not want to hear about what had happened to them. In his book, Frankl pointed out that it was a mistake to think that all the prisoners needed was to be freed; on the contrary, they needed emotional and spiritual support, perhaps now more than ever.

Although he identified the phases of camp life, Viktor Frankl was quick to point out that the phases did not determine all of a prisoner's reactions. He emphasized that the inmates had many opportunities to make choices as to how they responded to the things that were happening to them. He told a touching story about a young woman who lay dying in one of the camps. He thought readers might have a hard time believing the story. "But," he wrote, "to me it seems like a poem." The woman knew she was going to die. As Viktor sat beside her, she told him that before she was imprisoned, she had lived a luxurious, self-centered life. Now she was simply grateful for the single branch of a chestnut tree outside the window of the hut where she lay. She told him the tree was a friend to her and that she talked to it sometimes. Viktor wondered if she was delirious or hallucinating, so he asked if the tree spoke back to her. She told him, "Yes. . . . It said to me, 'I am here—I am here—I am life, eternal life.'" The young woman had chosen to look beyond her physical life, with all its former luxuries and present horrors, to know that life had a greater meaning.

In *Man's Search for Meaning*, Viktor Frankl identified the many tools prisoners found or created to help themselves stay alive. On Viktor's first night at Auschwitz, a former colleague came to him and the other men in his barracks. The man advised them that it was very important to look healthy, so that the SS officers would see them as people who could provide slave labor, instead of as candidates for the gas chamber. He told them one of the best things they could do was to shave every day, even if they had to do it with a piece of glass. He said that shaving would make them look younger and scraping their cheeks would give them a rosy, healthy-looking color. "If you want to stay alive," he said, "there is only one way: look fit for work."

It is hard to imagine finding a sense of humor in camps designed for death. But Viktor wrote, "Humor was another of the soul's weapons in the fight for self-preservation." He believed that humor can help us rise above a bad situation. He had a friend, another doctor, who was having a very difficult time coping with camp conditions. Viktor suggested that the two of them make up one story every day, imagining funny ways that camp life might affect them after they were free. The men were served watery soup every day. There might be a few peas or potatoes at the bottom of the kettle, so

A prisoner at Theresienstadt dishes out food, perhaps "from the bottom," to a newly arrived transport from the Netherlands. The rising steam, the white clothing, and the vacant look on the cook's face give him a ghostly appearance; it is as if the photo foretells what may lie in store for him.

if they dared, they would ask the server to give them "soup from the bottom." These few extra bites could mean the difference between life and death. Viktor and his friend made up one story in which they imagined attending a fancy dinner party after the war. When the hostess served the soup, they forgot where they were and asked for "soup from the bottom."

Perhaps the most important tool for survival came directly from logotherapy. It was a prisoner's belief in the meaning of his own life, no matter what was happening around him. Viktor himself used this tool over and over again, creating for himself dreams and goals for the future. He wrote, "The prisoner who had lost faith in the future—his future—was doomed." He told the story of a friend who had dreamed that the camp would be liberated on March 30, 1944. As the day approached and there were no signs of a liberating army nearby, the man grew more and more disappointed. When March 30 came and went and his situation had not changed, he completely gave up hope. He died on March 31. Viktor, on the other hand, was determined to keep his dreams alive—the dreams of seeing his mother and Tilly, of lecturing about the concentration camps and logotherapy. When prisoners were suicidal, he tried to get them to find a dream to live for. He often quoted Nietzsche: "He who has a *why* to live for can bear with almost any *how*."

The most basic tool of survival was simply putting survival before anything else—not only a person's own survival but also that of his or her friends. Viktor wrote that prisoners who served as cooks gave their friends soup from the bottom. Even though this meant Viktor often went hungrier if he was not a friend of the cook, he wrote that he couldn't blame someone for unfairness, because it was a matter of life and death for the cook's friends. With the compassion and acceptance Viktor would be known for, he wrote, "No man should judge unless he asks himself in absolute honesty whether in a similar situation he might not have done the same."

Besides analyzing the stages that a concentration camp prisoner experiences, Viktor also looked at the psychology of camp guards and Capos. Not long after the end of the war, people began asking how human beings could do the terrible things they had heard about. Viktor explained that some of the guards were true sadists, people who get pleasure from causing others to suffer. Sadists were assigned to perform torture and other especially horrific tasks. Guards who were not sadists had most often become numb to what they were seeing and doing, just as the prisoners had. Capos and other prisoners who worked in the gas chambers and crematoria received a ration of alcohol to help them stay numb.

Viktor also told about another group of guards, officers, and Capos. These were people who still had a conscience, who showed compassion at times. Viktor remembered a guard who saved him a piece of bread from his own rations. Viktor was moved to tears, not

In Man's Search for Meaning, Viktor analyzes the psychology of camp guards, as well as that of the prisoners. Here guards oversee new prisoners at Buchenwald Camp as they undress and put on uniforms after being selected to do slave labor.

so much by the gift of the bread as by what he called "the human 'something' which this man also gave to me—the word and look which accompanied the gift." He also remembered a Capo who helped him get a safer work detail and the barracks warden who arranged for Viktor to give an encouraging talk to the inmates.

There were larger kindnesses, too. The commander of the Türkheim camp actually used his own money to buy medicine for sick prisoners. When Viktor's group arrived at the camp, this commander expressed shock at the way the prisoners from Kaufering had been treated. When Türkheim was liberated, a group of Jewish prisoners hid the commander until they got a promise from the American troops that he would not be harmed. Viktor Frankl drew the conclusion:

> From all this we may learn that there are two races of men in this world, but only these two—the "race" of the decent man and the "race" of the indecent man. Both are found everywhere; they penetrate into all groups of society. No group consists entirely of decent or indecent people. In this sense, no group is of "pure race"—and therefore one occasionally found a decent fellow among the camp guards.

Over and over, Viktor's message in *Man's Search for Meaning* was presented clearly and powerfully: human beings, whether concentration camp prisoners or guards or people in the walk of everyday life, have a choice about how to respond to every situation they encounter. Viktor pointed out that it was not just camp conditions that shaped the prisoners' reactions. Rather, the inmates' personal decisions had as much to do with how they acted in camp as did the stresses of camp life. He wrote that in the camps, the prisoners saw some of their "comrades behave like swine while others behaved like saints. Man has both potentialities within himself; which one is actualized depends on decisions but not on conditions."

SIX

A TIME
TO LIVE

From the day of his birth until the summons to Sperlgymnasium that September day in 1942, Viktor Frankl's home had been the gray apartment building at Czerningasse 6 in the Vienna district of Leopoldstadt. Now the once-proud city of Vienna lay in ruins, and Leopoldstadt was ruled by the Soviet military. When people have been away from their hometown for a long time, often the first place they go when they return is their old neighborhood and their old home. For some reason, or maybe for many reasons, Viktor waited to revisit his former life. Maybe he dreaded what he would find there. His home might have been destroyed. The Frankl apartment might be occupied by people who gloated over what they had gained through his family's losses. Maybe all the family memories associated with the place would be too overwhelming, now that there was no one left to share them. And, practically speaking, it was sometimes difficult to move from one section to another in postwar Vienna, divided as it was among the four military powers.

Finally, Viktor took the step of crossing the Danube Canal into Leopoldstadt. The apartment building was still standing, and other people were now living in the Frankl flat. But neighbors and friends still lived at Viktor's old address, and he wanted to talk to some of them. One was Toni Grumbach, who had lived in an apartment below the Frankls. During the terrible destruction of Kristallnacht, Toni had made Viktor an offer. He said, "Viktor, you can come to me at any time and sleep in my flat. In that way maybe we can overcome these days of danger for Jewish people." Toni was a Brownshirt at the time, so he was able to provide some safety for Viktor. His offer supported Viktor's belief that there are good and bad people in every group.

Now it was Viktor's turn to be concerned about Toni. He knew that, as a former Nazi, Toni could be punished, and he wanted to know how he was. He knocked on the apartment door and was greeted by Toni's grandmother. She looked at Viktor suspiciously when he asked about Toni. She was afraid that anyone who came with questions about her grandson might be planning to turn him in to the authorities. She wouldn't tell Viktor anything about him.

There was someone else Viktor wanted to see, and whenever he thought of the man, Viktor felt an overpowering desire for revenge. During the year before the Frankls were deported, the Viennese were encouraged by the Nazis to wreak as much harm on their Jewish neighbors as they wished. Viktor would never say what the man had done, but he had been especially cruel to Frankl's mother. Whatever he said or did had affected her so deeply that she developed a heart problem after it happened. Viktor believed strongly that seeking revenge was wrong. But a person can feel something that is completely contradictory to what he believes.

He knocked on the door to the man's flat. Again, the door was answered by a grandmother. The first thing she told Viktor was that one of the man's legs had been amputated during the war. Maybe when he heard that, Viktor felt that the man had already been punished enough, or maybe his strong belief kept him from actually taking revenge. When he saw the man, he simply confronted him with words. He told him about his mother's heart problem and said, "And you caused this." He turned away from him then and hugged the man's grandmother. He couldn't make himself shake hands with the man himself. He left the apartment, his desire for revenge gone.

The Frankl family had stored a few small possessions with another person in the apartment building before they were deported, and Viktor's last task at Czerningasse 6 was to collect the items. Most of them meant something to Viktor but were not especially valuable otherwise. There were some books, a print by the Viennese artist Egon Schiele, Viktor's rock climbing rope, and his father's phylacteries. The phylacteries were very important to Viktor, and for the rest of his life, he used them when he prayed.

As he was finishing *Man's Search for Meaning*, Viktor Frankl began to think about Dr. Pitterman's suggestion that he return to work as a physician. In fact, Pitterman did more than suggest; he brought Viktor an application form and got him to fill it out. In February 1946, Viktor took a position as chief of neurology at the Vienna Policlinic Hospital, right across the street from his room on Mariannengasse.

Although he thought at times of emigrating to Australia, where his sister, Stella, lived, he cautiously began to put down roots in his home city. Over the years, many people questioned why he had

Beginning his return to normal life as chief of neurology at the Policlinic Hospital, Viktor demonstrates the use of logotherapy with a patient in the hospital lecture hall.

returned to Vienna. They asked, "Didn't they do enough to you in this city, to you and to your family?"

Viktor stubbornly refused to lump everyone in Vienna together. He reminded his questioners that a Catholic baroness in Vienna had hidden his cousin throughout the war. He told them about Dr. Pitterman, who had barely known Viktor before the war and had smuggled food to him whenever he could. By choosing to stay in Vienna, Viktor continued to live his belief that no group of people has a monopoly on good or evil.

Viktor had enjoyed the rewarding experience of delivering two books to his publisher, and he found his job satisfying. But he continued to be depressed, and he had a reputation at the hospital for being difficult to approach. Many of the people who found him inaccessible did not know that he was a concentration camp survivor and that his moodiness was due in part to his sorrow. Aside from the depression, however, Viktor, was naturally impatient when he thought that something that was obvious to him should also be obvious to others. It was not uncommon for him to express his irritation with sharp words, in a raised voice.

It happened one day that the oral surgery department needed a bed for a patient who had just had jaw surgery. The dental nursing staff thought there might be an extra bed on the neurology floor, but everyone was afraid to ask Dr. Frankl, who, as chief of neurology, would have to approve the loan of the bed. Twenty-year-old Eleonore Schwindt, an oral surgery assistant, was not intimidated, though. She volunteered for the task. The rest of the staff warned her, "Well, it's your neck, not ours." Elly stomped off in her huge soldier's boots, the only shoes she had been able to get during the war. A big white hospital coat with hugely stuffed pockets covered her compact, sturdy frame. She found Dr. Frankl making rounds on the basement level with a group of other doctors and medical students. Politely, she interrupted the discussion, using the form of address reserved for department heads: "Herr Primarius, excuse me. I am from the dental department and we have no bed for a patient just out of surgery. Is it possible to use a bed in your department?"

Dressed as she was, Elly must have looked a little odd, but the chief of neurology didn't notice her outlandish outfit. He saw only her warm, sparkling brown eyes. He looked into them steadily and almost forgot to speak, until Miss Schwindt started to think that *he* was a little odd. Remembering that he needed to respond, Dr. Frankl said, "Yes, of course. I'll arrange for the bed immediately."

*Viktor Frankl,
around 1947.*

Elly Schwindt returned to the oral surgery department with her news. The other nurses were amazed. "Did he shout at you?" "Was he angry about it?"

Elly said that it wasn't at all like that. "He was rather friendly about it. Quite a nice guy actually." Her friends were sure she couldn't be talking about the difficult Dr. Frankl.

Meanwhile, in the basement, Viktor turned to one of his assistants and said, "Did you see those eyes?" The incident turned out to be the beginning of Viktor Frankl and Elly Schwindt's courtship.

Viktor had been a prankster as a young boy, but Elly was at least as mischievous as he was, if not more so. As a little girl, she had loved to go up to the roof of the family deli and play a trick on people walking on the sidewalk below. She would tie a long, thin string to a little purse and let the purse lie on the sidewalk. When a passerby saw it and bent to pick it up, she quickly jerked the string and pulled the purse into the air. The greatest fun was watching people's reactions. Usually, they tried to pretend nothing had happened, that they hadn't been just about to take something that didn't belong to them.

Now her sense of humor helped to get the romance going between her and Viktor. The next time the two saw each other, Viktor told her he had a terrible toothache and also a terrible fear of dentists. He said the only way anyone would get him to see a dentist would be to lasso and drag him there. A few days later, Elly made a rope of gauze bandages, tied it into a lasso, and headed for Viktor's office. In the doorway, she whirled the lasso at the difficult chief of neurology and pretended she was going to capture him and haul him off to the dentist. Viktor had to confess that he didn't have a toothache and wasn't afraid of dentists. "I just needed an excuse to see you again," he said.

They talked for a while, and then Viktor asked Elly on a strange date. He wanted to know if she would like to come to his room to see a snake he had killed and preserved in a jar. They crossed the street to Viktor's poorly furnished room and looked at the snake, which was a very poisonous one Viktor had found while he was mountain climbing.

Viktor had fallen in love with Elly the instant he first looked into her dark eyes. For Elly, it took a little more time, but their friendship deepened. Viktor told Elly about his concentration camp experiences, about losing his family, and about his goals in life. He needed to talk, and she was a good listener. What attracted Elly to him most as he talked about his terrible ordeals was "the absence of bitterness and vengeance" in him. He worried, though, that she might be spending time with him because she felt sorry for him. After he expressed his fear, Elly wrote Viktor a note saying, "It is not pity, but love."

Elly was a very practical person, while Viktor was very intellectual. She knew that her practicality was something he needed. Later, she said, "Without me he would get lost in his own world, in his own thoughts." When Viktor came back to Vienna, he had been crushed to find that there was no one he loved waiting for him. Now he began to believe that that someone actually had been awaiting him, and that someone was Elly Schwindt.

Besides the lasting emotional effects the Holocaust had on survivors, it continued to impact their lives in unexpected, more mundane ways. As their relationship grew, Viktor and Elly decided they wanted to get married, but legally they couldn't. Viktor knew that Tilly had died at Bergen-Belsen, but the official notices of the millions of deaths in the camps took a long time to process. Without a death certificate, Viktor was legally still married to Tilly. Viktor and Elly decided that they would live together as husband and wife until they could actually marry, and she moved into Viktor's single room in 1946.

On July 16, 1947, Viktor received the notice of Tilly's death, and on July 18, 1947, Elly Schwindt and Viktor Frankl were married in a simple civil ceremony. Elly was Catholic, and Viktor was Jewish, so neither a Catholic priest nor a Jewish rabbi would agree to perform the ceremony.

Even though the war had been over for more than two years, Viktor and Elly were still very poor. Elly was proud of her new but inexpensive dress, bought for the wedding with carefully saved ration coupons. She had to wear her only pair of stockings, which were full of runs. Viktor wore the tie and a pair of women's shoes he had taken from Türkheim. Tilly's aunt, Grete Weiser, helped Viktor maintain his connection to Tilly's family by being his witness in the ceremony. At the wedding reception the newlyweds served "ice cream" that was made of water, sugar, and food coloring. There was no money for a honeymoon.

The Frankls continued to share their apartment with several other people. Elly's father found used furniture for them and carried it to their apartment in a wheelbarrow. He helped replace the cardboard in the windows with glass. As people gradually moved into their own homes, Elly and Viktor took over the apartment one room at a time.

In fact, one of the residents moved out just

Although Viktor knew of Tilly's death within a few months of his release from Türkheim, he did not get official word for more than two years. Here is a notice received by Viktor Stummer, a Viennese Jew who had escaped the Holocaust by immigrating to Shanghai, China. He waited for three years, only to hear that the fate of his relatives would probably never be known.

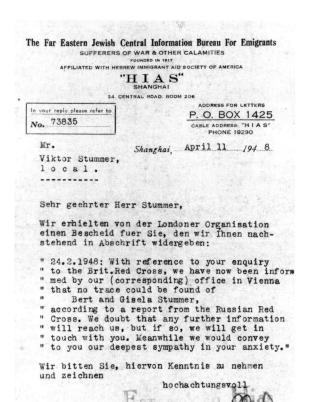

before December 14, 1947, so they had two rooms into which they could welcome their baby daughter, Gabriele. Beginning a new family was a very important way for concentration camp survivors to affirm that their lives were continuing. The birth of a child symbolized faith in a new life, not only for camp survivors but also for millions around the world who had lived through this terrible war. With his marriage to Elly and the birth of Gaby, Viktor Frankl, now forty-two, began to feel real joy in his new life. As they took over more of the flat, the corner room with its curved windows, Viktor's first home back in Vienna, became his study.

Elly had grown up in desperate poverty during the extremely difficult times between World War I and World War II, when her father was unemployed for nine years. She believed that that upbringing had molded her into the person she was when she met Viktor: a woman able to handle almost anything. Later, she would say, "It's not a problem if I have to clean windows or clean someone else's shoes. It's no problem if I have no money to buy meat or fancy things. If I have potatoes and bread, it's okay." Being poor, she said, had helped her to see what was truly essential in life.

Viktor and Elly's wedding; Viktor's witness, on the left, is Tilly's aunt.

This ability to see what was important in life had been especially important after the Anschluss. Elly was twelve years old then, and the Hitler Youth, the Nazi organization for young people, offered many incentives to get young people to join. Many of them, hungry and poor, became part of the movement when they were offered food or work with pay. Elly was not at all drawn to Hitler, but she said the rewards of participating might have tempted her if her father had not made his values clear; she knew he would not tolerate her signing up.

Because she had grown up in a cramped two-room apartment with her parents and brother, Elly's one great wish when she married Viktor was to have a room of her own. When more rooms became available, she got her wish, and eventually the whole apartment belonged to the new Frankl family.

Viktor lost no time introducing Elly to his great love—mountain climbing. She didn't like it at first, but she never missed a climbing session. She said, "It was never my dream to do rock climbing. But I thought, If I go with him, he must stop where I'm not capable of doing harder things. So he stopped. I did it to protect him. Of course I was always proud when I arrived at the top."

The Frankls most often climbed in Austria but also ascended peaks in Italy, South Africa, and at Yosemite in the United States. Three different trails on two Austrian mountains have been named after Viktor. Once Don Klingberg, Viktor's biographer, asked an old Viennese man if he knew who Viktor Frankl was. "But of course!" the old man replied. "The mountain climber!"

As more and more people read *Man's Search for Meaning*, the Frankl apartment became the heart of the logotherapy movement. Around twenty-five letters a day poured into their home. Elly quickly became part of Viktor's work. The two of them read all the mail together, and together they decided how to answer it. Before

Viktor left in the morning, he dictated correspondence, and Elly took shorthand. While he worked at the hospital, she typed the letters, then brought them to him to sign.

One day Viktor set some pages of English text in front of Elly. When she objected that she didn't know English, Viktor immediately became impatient; he had learned English earlier in his life and couldn't see why Elly shouldn't master it just by having the English letters in front of her. Elly met Viktor's challenge, and that was how she began learning English—pecking it out on the typewriter, one letter at a time.

Viktor spent his afternoons at home, writing books, preparing lectures, and answering more mail. Many of the letters requested lectures, and he and Elly began to travel to speaking platforms around the world. Once Elly joked, "The meaning of logotherapy is work," and the joke became a standard in the Frankl family.

Before Gaby started kindergarten, Elly felt pulled in many directions. She wanted to spend time with Gaby, and she needed to do housework and grocery shopping, and in the middle of all that were the huge and growing demands of getting logotherapy out into the world. She worried that the work of logotherapy might cheat Gaby out of the attention she needed from her mother and father. But Gaby said later that she felt she had gotten more attention from her parents than most children did. When Viktor was not traveling, he spent time talking to her, and he was a wonderful storyteller, bringing Gaby into the magical world of myths and legends. Viktor, Elly, and Gaby spent many weekends together on Rax Mountain. They went pic-

Climbing Rax Mountain in the 1950s.

nicking and swimming in the Old Danube River and watched live outdoor wrestling matches in the part of Vienna where Elly had grown up. When Gaby got a good report card, she could run across the street to the Policlinic to show her father. The staff always received her warmly, and they let her in to see him as soon as he was finished taking care of the patient he was with.

Anti-Semitism did not leave Vienna with the end of the Nazi era. One day, a teacher of Gaby's made some prejudiced statements about Jews. When Gaby told Viktor and Elly about it, Viktor decided it was time to help Gaby develop a different sense of what it meant to be Jewish. He began to consciously point out positive Jewish role models to her. When guests visited and Viktor noticed Gaby admiring them, he would tell her later, "And you know, Gaby, that these people were Jewish." He wanted her to believe "that Jews are good people."

Viktor and Elly's daughter Gabriele at age three.

Family was always very important to Viktor, and the small family he and Elly created after the war became a source of strength for him. Their home in Vienna was a place to which Viktor could return from his work in the world and receive support and find renewal. Because of the demands of their work, he and Elly decided not to have more children after Gaby was born, and they kept their family life very private.

Gaby grew up to study psychology. She chose to specialize in child development rather than logotherapy. It was important for her to make her own way, a little separate from her famous father. In 1969, she married Franz Vesely, who was then a PhD student in physics. Gaby and Franz had two children, Katharina and Alexander. Their grandchildren were very special to Viktor and Elly and brought them a lot of pleasure. When they were born, Viktor was still busy lecturing and writing, but he had retired from the Policlinic, and he had even more time for his grandchildren than he had had for Gaby, so they became very close.

Over the years, many people had been critical of the Frankls' interfaith marriage, but Viktor and Elly themselves moved easily between Catholic and Jewish traditions. Each respected the other's faith and celebrated the other's customs. They attended services in both synagogue and church, sometimes separately and at other times together or with Gaby and their grandchildren. They celebrated Chanukah and Christmas, and on those days they ate a simple meal of potato soup as a reminder "that others were in danger and in need" and to remember "their own former desperation."

In 1977, thirty years after their civil wedding ceremony, Viktor and Elly wanted to have a religious ceremony. They hoped that attitudes had changed and that both a priest and a rabbi could now bless their long marriage. A Catholic cardinal approved the ceremony, but the chief rabbi of Vienna would not agree. Viktor let go of the idea then, saying, "It was no longer *our* problem."

Besides lecturing, writing, and mountain climbing, the Frankls socialized with family and friends from many walks of life. There were other physicians from the Policlinic; the widow of Viktor's old friend Hubert Gsur, who took him to the mountains when it was against the law; Tilly's aunt; Elly's father and mother; Viktor and Elly's mountain-climbing friends; and, more and more frequently, logotherapists and others interested in logotherapy from around the world. The Frankls' lives had become rich with people and work.

Viktor loved to tell jokes; some he told many times. One of his favorites was about two Israeli soldiers who are told that, unexpectedly, they need to parachute out of their plane because it is not going to stop where they need to get off. They will be parachuting into the desert, but the pilot tells them not to worry because he has radioed ahead for a jeep to meet them. The soldiers make the jump, but neither one can get his parachute to open. They're falling faster and faster toward the earth, and one says to the other, "Now watch. When we reach the ground, there won't be any jeep to meet us, either!"

Viktor could also be romantic and dramatic, not worrying what other people might think. One time when he and Elly were visiting New York City, they stayed at a hotel not far from the airport. After they checked their luggage, they took a walk to a neighborhood synagogue. On the way, Viktor started to sing "Strangers in the Night." He grabbed Elly and danced down the sidewalk with her, accompanied by his own singing.

Viktor was a man of many interests, and he had the necessary energy to pursue them. Like his sister, Stella, he was keenly interested in fashion. He loved neckties and loved to window-shop for them, as well as to buy them. He had become so well informed about styles of eyeglasses that a large manufacturer of frames brought sketches of new designs to Viktor so he could give his opinion before they went into production. He wrote music, too—an elegy, which was played by a symphony orchestra, and a tango, which was used in a television program.

He also wrote a play about his experiences in the camps. One act of the play was performed in Toronto, Canada, as an introduction to one of his lectures there. At the performance, Viktor had the odd experience of being what he called "the 'third' Viktor Frankl." The first Frankl was an actor playing Viktor as a concentration camp inmate, and the second was a narrator, another an actor playing Viktor Frankl. The third Frankl was himself, sitting in the audience.

Viktor loved to collect autographs, and he wasn't at all shy about asking for them. He once went up to a famous Austrian wrestler in a café in Vienna and asked for his autograph. He got the signature of Captain Kangaroo, a children's TV personality in America from the 1950s to the 1980s. He loved watching children's television, especially the Muppets, when he was in the United States. Because he had a big chest and spindly legs, he called himself Kermit the Frog. He called his sister, Stella, who was taller and heavier than he was, Big Bird. Despite the terrible things that had happened to him, Viktor had the wonderful ability, no matter how old he got, to keep the child within him vibrantly alive.

Together, Viktor, Elly, and Gaby Frankl had transformed their corner of war-ravaged Vienna into a home that was filled with life. It was certainly a life of developing and sharing logotherapy around the world. It was also marked by a shared passion for simple daily pleasures. The Frankl home reflected the way Viktor met and drank from every experience—whether it was challenging his body and

Viktor's granddaughter, Katharina, chats with him while he takes a break from dictating in his home office.

mind on a mountaintop or dragging an American friend into a coffee shop and commanding, "Smell! Freshly ground Viennese coffee." To Viktor Frankl, who had come so close to dying in the camps and had afterward considered suicide, life had become a most precious gift, one to be embraced to the fullest. As Elly put it, "When I met him, he was a depressed person. And, step by step, he became like a boy. He could laugh like a ten-year-old boy."

Eleven

THE WORLD RESPONDS

One morning at three o'clock, the phone jangled Viktor Frankl awake. The woman on the line had called because she had decided to kill herself, but before she did, she wanted to hear what Dr. Frankl might have to say about it. He talked with her for half an hour about her choice. Often he told patients that people who tried to commit suicide and failed were usually grateful afterward that they hadn't been successful. Maybe that was one of the arguments he used with her. At any rate, he gave her many reasons against killing herself. At last she agreed to come and see him at nine o'clock that morning. When she reached Dr. Frankl's office, she told him it wasn't the arguments that had helped her. She had come because, even when he'd been awakened in the middle of the night,

Frankl had listened patiently and encouraged her. She was so touched by the humanness of this experience that she thought it might "be worthwhile to give my life another chance." Viktor talked about his experience with this patient to illustrate that when someone is trying to help people who are discouraged, showing human caring and kindness is far more important than the theories or techniques a person uses.

At the Policlinic, Dr. Frankl extended himself with kindness and concern that were easily felt by his patients. Sometimes his kindness included a dose of toughness, as he challenged his patients to rise above their situations. An important principle in logotherapy is the acceptance of personal responsibility, and patients who were looking for sympathy did not necessarily want to be expected to make an effort on their own behalf.

An American doctor visited Viktor in his office once. The doctor wanted Frankl to tell him the difference between psychoanalysis and logotherapy. Viktor asked the doctor to describe psychoanalysis. The doctor answered, "During psychoanalysis, the patient must lie down on a couch and tell you things which sometimes are very disagreeable to tell." Viktor, with his characteristic sense of humor, but also quite seriously, said, "Now, in logotherapy the patient may remain sitting erect but he must hear things which sometimes are very disagreeable to hear."

Sometimes, Dr. Frankl's patients found his challenges uncomfortable because they required change and the hard work that goes with it. For example, a patient would certainly like to overcome depression. A depressed patient seeking help through psychoanalysis might spend years telling the psychotherapist all the unhappy events of his childhood. A depressed patient seeking help through logotherapy might hear the therapist tell her she needs to actively go out and volunteer in a hospital or start taking courses at the uni-

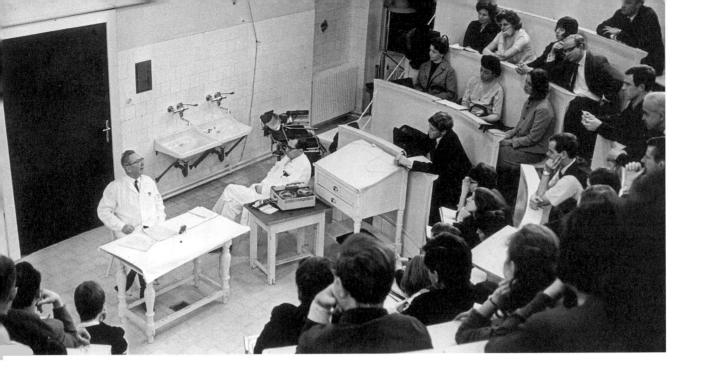

Viktor gives what was known as a "Wednesday lecture" at the Policlinic.

versity. It can feel almost impossible for a depressed person to do something as simple as getting out of bed in the morning. So, although working toward a goal might very well alleviate the patient's depression, it could also be very challenging to take the first step.

At other times, patients experienced great relief when they heard Dr. Frankl's suggestions. One day a fellow doctor came to him as a patient. The man was still overwhelmed with grief after the death of his wife two years earlier. Dr. Frankl asked him what would have happened if the doctor had died and his wife had lived. The man answered that she would have suffered terribly if she had lost him. Viktor suggested that because his wife had died first, the doctor was now sparing his beloved that terrible suffering. The suggestion brought peace to the doctor's heart, and he left the office with a calm he had not felt for months. Frankl wrote that suffering is no longer suffering "at the moment it finds a meaning, such as the meaning of a sacrifice."

Besides compassion, toughness, and a sense of humor, Viktor

brought to his practice a keen ability to perceive more than what his patients presented on the surface. He thought this ability might be related to his talent as a caricature artist. Caricaturists look for an outstanding characteristic in their subject, often a weakness, such as a bulbous nose or large ears. Then they emphasize that weakness in their drawings. As a caricaturist, Viktor became adept at spotting people's physical weaknesses. As a psychiatrist, he was good at spotting people's mental and emotional vulnerabilities. But even more important to him and his patients, he was good at seeing the possibilities for overcoming their shortcomings.

In a sense, the people who read *Man's Search for Meaning* also became Viktor's patients, as his book helped them find meaning in painful life situations and enabled them to face those situations with courage. A psychology professor who requires that his students read the book reports that some of them have said it stopped them from considering suicide. One student who had a terminal illness "took heart that his life, which was to end so early, could still be filled with meaning as he tried to help others in their need." A political prisoner in Asia told a *Newsweek* reporter that he had survived his prison experience because his mother had sent him *Man's Search for Meaning*. He said, "And that book keeps me going."

Jerry Long, a young man whose arms and legs were paralyzed in a car accident, wrote to Dr. Frankl after he read *Man's Search for Meaning*. He said he felt his suffering was less severe than Viktor's had been and that the book had inspired him because he knew Viktor had lived what he taught. Later, Jerry met Frankl and told him, "The accident broke my back, but it did not break me."

Viktor made fun of himself as well as others in his caricatures. This one, drawn on a napkin, appeared in a Tokyo newspaper in 1969.

＜自画像＞演説するフランクル博士

A young Israeli soldier lost both of his legs after the Yom Kippur War in 1973. He couldn't imagine life without his legs, and he began to think of suicide. One day, the psychologist who had been treating him went into the soldier's hospital room and found him a changed person. When she asked what had happened, he showed her *Man's Search for Meaning* and said, "This book is what happened to me."

Once, in the middle of a busy lecture tour in Northern California, Viktor was handed a note by a prison official. The note was from an inmate who had read *Man's Search for Meaning* in the San Quentin prison library. He asked if Dr. Frankl would consider visiting him at the prison. Viktor agreed immediately, although the sponsors of the tour weren't very happy about having to rearrange his tight schedule. His host drove him north along the San Francisco Bay to the massive cream-colored prison built on a rocky outcropping. Inside San Quentin, Viktor ended up speaking to a whole group of prisoners. He had often said that with freedom comes responsibility. He told the men, "You were free to commit a crime, to become guilty. Now, however, you are responsible for overcoming guilt by rising above it, by growing beyond yourselves, by changing for the better."

Often, famous people wanted to meet Viktor Frankl after they learned about him. One of Viktor and Elly's greatest honors came when Pope Paul VI invited them to an audience. Usually people request an audience with the pope, but this time it was the other way around. The pope spoke with them through an interpreter for almost twenty minutes. He said that logotherapy had been important to people in the Catholic Church and mentioned Viktor's experiences in the concentration camps and his accomplishments as a logotherapist. At the end of the interview, the pope spoke in German, asking Viktor, "Please pray for me!" Viktor was moved

Viktor and Elly meet with Pope Paul VI in 1970.

that the pope, the head of the Catholic Church, would ask him, "a Jewish neurologist from Vienna," to pray for him.

As *Man's Search for Meaning* gained wider influence, Viktor was frequently invited to lecture around the world. He was a dynamic, fascinating lecturer who used a chalkboard as if it were his speaking partner. Sometimes, he illustrated his talks with slide shows depicting the giants on whose shoulders he stood—Freud and Adler, and others. He used examples and stories from daily life to illustrate the points he was making. The stories often brought laughter and tears to his audience.

Viktor liked to bring ideas from mountain climbing into his lectures. When he was sixty-seven years old, he took his first flying lessons. After he earned his pilot's license, he also liked to include experiences from flying in his talks. In a 1973 lecture before the Toronto Youth Corps, he told how, in a crosswind, a pilot must aim the plane higher, or farther north, than his goal in order to reach his actual destination. He said that it was like this with human beings. If we expect something higher of ourselves, we will reach what we are actually capable of. If we aim only for what we are capable of, we are likely to achieve beneath our abilities.

Sometimes, this man who loved heights referred to logotherapy as "height psychology." He contrasted it with depth psychology, which probes deeply into people's unconscious minds to find out what might be wrong there. Height psychology, on the other hand, encourages people to focus on the best and the highest in themselves and to strive to make their ideals a reality.

Although he received invitations to lecture around the world, not all responses to Viktor and his work were positive. He often took strong stands that were sometimes unpopular. Right after the war, in 1946, he was already speaking out against the idea of *collective guilt*. People who believed in collective guilt thought that all members of a particular group were responsible for what other members of the group had done. In the case of the Holocaust, they held all Germans responsible for the actions of the German government and armies during the war. Some even believed that German children who had not been born at the time of the war were as guilty as their parents. Moreover, they held all members of the Nazi party equally responsible for things that only certain Nazis had done. People who believed in collective guilt became very angry about Viktor's insistence that everyone is individually responsible for his or her own actions. Many of these people were themselves survivors of the Holocaust or had lost their families, just as Viktor had. Other survivors, including Elie Wiesel, the well-known author and speaker on the Holocaust, agreed with Viktor.

There was a time when Viktor's stand on collective guilt was such a sore point that people almost resorted to violence against him. In 1978, Viktor was invited to be one of the speakers in a series of lec-

Viktor with his flying instructor. He was very proud of his pilot's license, which hangs on a wall in his home alongside his Alpine guide certificate and his academic awards.

tures at a Jewish temple in New York. He talked about his experiences during the Holocaust. When he started to talk about the kind things some Viennese citizens had done for him, he felt the audience begin to grow restless. Some of those citizens, like Dr. Pötzl, who had helped him save Jewish lives, had even become Nazis. The audience became more and more upset. They didn't want to hear that there could have been some good in people who were part of something as evil as the Nazi government. At last, when Viktor mentioned Bruno Kreisky, a Jewish leader who had a reputation for possibly having worked with the Nazis, some of the crowd became enraged. They stood up and booed, shook their fists, and called Viktor a "Nazi pig." Elly was sitting in the audience and felt the waves of overpowering rage all around her. She grew more and more frightened that the people might even kill Viktor.

The rabbi who was hosting the lecture went to the microphone and asked those who didn't want to listen to leave. Many did go, but the majority stayed and heard Viktor out. After his lecture, they discussed his ideas respectfully. Viktor had spoken in many highly charged situations—in front of a Nazi Brownshirt just before Hitler took over Austria, with a Gestapo officer when his life was on the line, and in concentration camp barracks—but having his own people be so furious with him hurt him deeply. Nevertheless, he continued to stand by his belief that individuals are responsible only for their own actions and not for the actions of others.

Many Holocaust survivors and other Jews who had been profoundly affected by the Holocaust found it difficult to accept Frankl's broad tolerance. They felt that he should want to repay those who had hurt him, as many of them did. Since he didn't, they concluded that he had sided with the Nazis. Except for the one time when he went back to his old apartment, Viktor refused to let himself be motivated by revenge. At the same time, he refused to judge people who felt a need for retribution. As time healed some of the wounds from the Holocaust, many more people came to think as Viktor did. With healing, they were able to embrace the tolerance he had advocated from the beginning.

While some felt that Viktor's attitude was too lenient, others thought he spoke too much about the Holocaust. Viktor, however, felt that it was very important to remind people of what had happened. Sometimes, both Jews and non-Jews would ask, "Why bring up this Holocaust business over and over? . . . Why not allow the pain to go away?" Viktor answered, "Forgetting something like this deprives us of the chance to see to it that it never is repeated."

Others accused Frankl of using his experiences during the Holocaust to promote himself and logotherapy, especially in *Man's Search for Meaning*. They suggested, for example, that his book claimed that having a positive mental attitude might enable a person to survive anything, even something as terrible as the Holocaust. They reasoned that such a claim promoted logotherapy as the only tool a prisoner would have needed to survive; they further reasoned that if *Man's Search for Meaning* promoted logotherapy, it also promoted Viktor Frankl as its founder. On the contrary, Viktor was very careful to say that in the camps death was often inevitable. People could not change that fact; they could, however, change how they faced their death. He wrote about the dignity of the person who "entered those gas chambers upright, with the Lord's Prayer or the Shema Yisrael on his lips."

Viktor also showed that there were many chance events, having nothing to do with his own mental attitude, that had saved his life. As an example, he told of a time when he worked under an especially brutal Capo who had chosen him as his beating victim that day. Viktor was getting more and more exhausted, thinking he couldn't make it much longer, when an air-raid siren pierced the air. The prisoners had to be regrouped after that, and Viktor was placed under a different Capo. He wrote that if this had not happened, he would probably have been brought back "to camp on one of the sledges which carried those who had died or were dying from exhaustion." In this case, it was the shrilling of the siren that saved him, not a positive attitude or a focus on finding meaning in the situation.

Viktor pointed out early in *Man's Search for Meaning*, "We who have come back, by the aid of many lucky chances or miracles—whatever one may choose to call them—we know: the best of us did not return." People who were actually there in the concentration camps with Viktor did not share the criticisms of some of his readers. Two of his fellow prisoners told their doctor soon after the war, "Viktor Frankl was always trying to find ways to help [us] and other prisoners in the camps . . . even then he was the same man."

Despite the fact that *Man's Search for Meaning* has been described as the second-most widely read book about the Holocaust after *The Diary of Anne Frank*, as late as 1995 it could not be found on the shelves of the bookstore in the United States Holocaust Memorial Museum in Washington, D.C. The omission of Frankl's book seems to point to the depth of the controversies surrounding his account. Gradually, attitudes toward Viktor and his work have changed among the people most affected by the Holocaust, and this is evidenced in part by the fact that by 2000 *Man's Search for Meaning* had found a place on the museum's bookshelves.

Readers were not only critical of Viktor's stubborn refusal to embrace the idea of collective guilt; many also had difficulty understanding how Viktor could be open to so many religions besides his own. They were disturbed by the fact that he had married a Catholic woman. They were critical of Frankl because logotherapy's emphasis on meaning and suprameaning and on rising above difficult situations appealed to Christian psychotherapists. Many of these psychotherapists wrote books and articles about how logotherapy fit with Christian thinking and how they had used it with Christian patients. Some of Frankl's critics felt that because Christian psychotherapists so readily adopted logotherapy, Viktor wasn't "Jewish enough."

Other critics thought logotherapy wasn't psychotherapy at all, that it *was* a religion. Viktor insisted that psychotherapy, including logotherapy, was separate from religion. He said that the two had very different goals. "Psychotherapy aims at mental health. Religion aims at salvation." On the other hand, Frankl acknowledged that religion could help with a patient's mental healing. He had also seen that psychotherapy often made patients aware of the spiritual part of themselves. However, he insisted that good psychotherapists, whether or not they were religious, must keep religion out of treatment in order to be available to all patients who came to them for help, regardless of their beliefs.

Freud's followers, the psychoanalysts, continued to disparage Viktor's work, quite possibly because he remained very critical of psychoanalysis, despite his admiration for Freud as a great thinker. Frankl openly criticized the psychoanalysts' emphasis on people's weaknesses rather than their strengths, and the high fees many of them charged their patients for years of therapy, often with few results.

The conflict between the two schools of psychotherapy was talked about enough at home that even as a young child, Gaby Frankl was quite aware of it. One day, she went along with her father to the Vienna airport. He was flying to London to speak. Before he boarded the plane, Gaby looked up at him and said, "Please, papa. Speak loudly and clearly, and take care that your airplane will not be shot by your enemies, the psychoanalysts."

Viktor in the apartment on Mariannengasse, where he lived for fifty-two years, in the room that now houses the Viktor Frankl Archives. On the shelves are some of his many publications, and on the wall a few of his awards.

The response to Viktor Frankl's contributions to psychotherapy was mixed in the academic world of colleges and universities. He became a lecturer at the University of Vienna soon after the publication of *The Doctor and the Soul*, but he was never promoted to a full professorship there. However, he was frequently asked to lecture at universities around the world, including Harvard, Yale, and the University of California at Los Angeles.

It is difficult to say why Viktor seemed to be more highly thought of in academic circles outside Vienna than he was at home. It has been suggested that professional jealousy might have kept him from advancing at the university. However, Frankl's personal style may also have contributed to the way his colleagues and supervisors related to him. He has been described as "paradoxically dogmatic and open, strident and gracious," authoritarian and tolerant in professional situations.

In keeping with his belief that each human being has a unique purpose to accomplish, Viktor believed that his life had been spared against all odds because he had a destiny to fulfill. Because of his powerful belief that it was his responsibility to present logotherapy to the world, he often spoke forcefully, sometimes even arrogantly. There were times when he felt that others did not recognize the importance of logotherapy, and he became defensive, citing the number of his books sold and the volume of letters he received every day. What Viktor saw as his responsibility to bring logotherapy to the world could be seen by some colleagues as self-promoting and may have alienated some of them.

At the Policlinic, Dr. Frankl not only saw his own patients, he also taught young doctors and medical students in neurology and psychiatry. Some of his students became well known as logotherapists in Sweden, Germany, and Austria. They lectured in other countries and wrote books about their research. Today there are logotherapy training and therapy institutes and archives in thirty-one countries. Logotherapy has been especially well received in Central and South America, where there are a total of twenty-seven logotherapy institutes in ten nations. New articles, books, and films on Viktor Frankl and logotherapy continue to be published; since 2003, fifty-one books have been published in seventeen countries, some of them reprintings of Viktor's own work. Others are the work of scholars who follow in his footsteps.

Logotherapy is recognized by the American Medical Association, the American Psychiatric Association, and the American Psychological Association as one of the scientifically based schools of psychotherapy, and there are two logotherapy training institutes and an archive of original Frankl papers in the United States. In 2005, professional researchers and psychotherapists met at the Fifteenth World Congress on Logotherapy in Dallas, Texas, to present papers on the most recent logotherapeutic studies. Logotherapy has also influenced newer psychotherapy treatments. For example, Canadian psychologist Paul T. P. Wong has said that Viktor Frankl should be recognized as the father of the contemporary practice of positive psychology, which emphasizes working with the strengths people bring to life's difficult situations. Positive psychology founder Martin Seligman names a *meaningful life* as one of three kinds of happy lives; the other two are the *pleasant life* and the *good life*. The work that Viktor began when he was in high school continues to grow and to help people find meaning in their lives on every inhabited continent in the world.

Eight

**SAYING YES
UNTIL THE END**

In the Old City of Jerusalem, in the land of Israel, there stands an ancient wall built of cream-colored stone. Small, dark shrubs grow out of cracks between the huge blocks of rock. Other cracks are stuffed with pieces of paper that have prayers written on them. From dawn until dusk, hundreds of people rock back and forth in front of the wall, some touching their foreheads to it, praying and grieving for the destruction of the Jewish temple by the Romans in the year 70 C.E. (Common Era, also referred to as A.D.) The Western Wall is more than two thousand years old. It is the only standing wall of the temple built by King Herod the Great, in the first century B.C.E. (Before the Common Era, also referred to as B.C.) Today, it is one of the most sacred places in Judaism. From all

127

over the world, people come to pray and to celebrate Jewish holidays and special life events.

When he was thirteen, Viktor Frankl was declared a man at his bar mitzvah ceremony in a Vienna synagogue. At eighty-three, he chose to celebrate a second bar mitzvah at the Western Wall in Jerusalem. It is a joyful time in Jewish tradition when someone has lived seventy years beyond his first bar mitzvah at thirteen and chooses to celebrate his commitment to Jewish law and life once again. Wearing his prayer shawl and his father's phylacteries, Viktor listened and repeated the sacred texts with the rabbi. As the rabbi went on, Viktor kept saying to himself, "How beautiful, how beautiful."

Viktor Frankl's second bar mitzvah was only one indication of the depth of his commitment to his faith. He didn't often talk about it because he felt that faith is something private. But from the time of his release from Türkheim, he prayed the Shema Yisrael every day. He also prayed his own prayers. After the Holocaust, if something bad happened to him, he imagined himself on his knees and gave thanks "to heaven that this is the worst thing that happened to me today."

Viktor in Jerusalem for his second bar mitzvah, with the Western Wall behind him. To his right is the late Dr. Mignon Eisenberg and to his left, Professor David Guttmann. Together, the two arranged Viktor's visit and bar mitzvah. The bearded man is the rabbi, known simply as The Rabbi of the Wall.

After his losses and the horrors he suffered in the Holocaust, Viktor Frankl allowed himself to get irritated about life's small annoyances, but he refused to complain about the big problems that came his way. For example, once when he was staying at an Alpine lodge, planning an early morning climb, people in the bar below were having a loud party. Viktor finally went downstairs and yelled at them to be quiet so he could get some sleep. However, even when he became blind at the age of eighty-five, as Elly said, "Viktor lived what he talked—absolutely. . . . Never did he complain about his blindness. Not even once."

Blindness struck suddenly one evening when he was watching TV. Elly was working in the kitchen, and suddenly, she heard him calling her. When she got to the living room, he said simply, "Elly, I am blind." For the next seven years, Viktor would be able to see only dim shapes with one eye, and nothing with the other. Despite his blindness, he continued to write and lecture.

Although much of Frankl's lecturing took place around the world, he was also asked to speak on special occasions in his hometown. One evening, two years after he went blind, Viktor spoke in Leopoldstadt, where he had played in the Prater, attended Sperlgymnasium, had his first bar mitzvah, and lived with Tilly and his parents. In a lecture hall a few blocks from his former home, he spoke on the topic "Up to the Time of Deportation to the Concentration Camps." He talked about his early life and about how the Holocaust had arrived in Leopoldstadt. His old neighbor, Toni Grumbach, who had offered to hide Viktor, was at the lecture. Viktor had had a chance, after the time he talked with Toni's grandmother at the Czernigasse apartment, to thank Toni privately; now he did so publicly. People Viktor had never met came to ask if he had ever seen this friend or that relative of theirs in the camps. After all this time, they were still hungry for any information they could get about their loved ones. One woman at the lecture had known Viktor at Theresienstadt, and she thanked him for helping to keep her and others there from committing suicide.

Elly and Viktor had been partners in the work of bringing logotherapy to the world throughout their marriage. Now that he was blind, Viktor depended on Elly more than ever. Viktor had earned a PhD in addition to his MD at the University of Vienna, and many universities had awarded him honorary doctoral degrees in recognition of his contributions. In 1993, North Park University in Chicago wanted to grant honorary doctorates to both Viktor and Elly. This was the first time an institution had recognized Elly's contributions, so Viktor refused the award for himself. He wanted the entire honor to go to Elly this time, because without her work and loving support, he would not have been able to accomplish the things he had. While Elly was receiving a standing ovation from the crowd, Viktor did something that wasn't on the program: he walked up to her from backstage without help. She started to cry when she saw him coming, and when he got to her, he took her head in his hands and kissed away her tears.

Joseph Fabry, an American logotherapist born in Vienna, translated Viktor's autobiography, *Recollections*, into English with his wife, Judith. He also founded the first Institute of Logotherapy in the United States. In his foreword to *Recollections*, he painted a word portrait of four different Viktors he had gotten to know. The first Viktor Frankl was the one he got acquainted with during Viktor's lecture tours in California. Fabry said that on tour, Viktor was under tremendous pressure to keep up with a demanding schedule and wouldn't even stop to visit over a cup of coffee or to eat a nice meal in a restaurant.

At home in Vienna, Fabry met the second Viktor Frankl. There, Fabry wrote, "Frankl is a different man." Although Viktor was still

Viktor continued rock climbing until he was eighty, when worsening eyesight forced him to quit. Here he is pictured at age seventy.

extremely busy in Vienna, he took the opportunity there to enjoy life. Fabry was the friend Viktor had pulled into a coffee shop one day and ordered him to "Smell!" On that same walk, Viktor drew him into a bakery and said again, "Smell, freshly baked Viennese rolls."

The second Viktor Frankl generously gave of his time to ordinary people. Stefan, a high school student from Graz, a city south of Vienna, wrote to Viktor about how *Man's Search for Meaning* had helped him overcome his grief when his father died. After he read the book, he gave a presentation on Viktor Frankl in his class. His fellow students were intensely interested in the Frankl story. Maybe Stefan reminded Viktor of himself and the presentations he had made at that age at Sperlgymnasium. In any case, after Viktor and Elly read his letter, they called Stefan, invited him to visit them in Vienna, and spent a whole afternoon talking with him.

The third Viktor Frankl could be seen rapidly scaling the sheer rock walls of Rax Mountain with the graceful movements he was known for. He loved breathing the mountain air and letting the beauty of the peaks and meadows touch his spirit. On the summits, he could forget about his next book or lecture and just enjoy the moment. He found solitude there and wrote, "Every important decision I have made, almost without exception, I have made in the mountains."

Finally, Fabry said, there was Viktor Frankl the prophet. Another name for a prophet is *seer,* because prophets see things that others haven't seen, or they see them in a different way. One of a prophet's tasks is to warn the world of the things he or she has seen. Viktor Frankl spent much of his life "warning against the horrors of a meaningless life, an empty or frustrated life." As a student from Berkeley, who was visiting Vienna, once said to Dr. Frankl, "The meaning of your life is to help others find the meaning of theirs."

In October 1996, Viktor answered the phone in his study, and after he hung up, Elly heard an outcry from his room. His niece had just told him that his sister, Stella, had died in Australia. That evening, Viktor was admitted to the hospital. He had already been in the hospital several times for heart problems. But after Stella died, his health seemed to get much worse. He finally decided, at the age of ninety-two, to have heart surgery, even though he and his family knew that he would probably not survive it.

While he was in the hospital, Elly brought his phylacteries to him every day and stood outside the closed door of his room to make sure he would have privacy for his prayers. On the morning of his surgery, he told Elly, "I have inscribed one of my books to you and I have hidden it in our apartment. There you will find it." Then he whispered to her, "I want to thank you once more, Elly, for all that you have done for me in your life."

Viktor did not regain consciousness after his surgery. For three days he was in the intensive care unit. During that time Elly held earphones to his ears so that he could hear a cassette tape his grandson, Alexander, had made for him. On the tape, Alexander had put some of Viktor's favorite music by Mozart and Gustav Mahler. That is how Viktor Frankl spent the last three days of his life, with Elly at his side. He died on September 2, 1997.

In keeping with Jewish tradition, Viktor was buried immediately after his death. The family was offered a place of honor where Viktor could be buried in Vienna's Central Cemetery. But Viktor had already chosen to be buried in the family plot in the old Jewish part of the cemetery. In the words of Alexander, "He wanted to be buried the way he was born, somebody not known to the world, in a very simple way." Viktor's grave is beneath the headstone where his maternal grandmother is buried. The names of his parents, Elsa and Gabriel, and his brother and sister-in-law, Walter and Else Frankl, have been added to the headstone in memory of those who perished in the Holocaust. Beneath that are the words VIKTOR EMIL FRANKL, 26.MÄRZ 1905–2.SEPTEMBER 1997. Nothing is written there about all his accomplishments and awards. And yet there is a silent reminder of the many lives Viktor Frankl touched: the marker is

A 1994 portrait by
Viktor's granddaughter,
Katharina.

covered with smooth round pebbles. By Jewish custom, small stones are placed at the gravesite by those who wish to honor the person who has died.

After Viktor was gone, Elly searched the apartment for the hidden book he had told her about. Finally, one day when she was dusting the books in his study, she found *Homo Patiens (Suffering Man)*, which seemed to have slipped behind the others. Elly pulled it forward and opened it. When the book was published, Viktor had dedicated it to Elly with one word: Elly. Now Elly saw that above her printed name, Viktor had written the word For. Below it, he had written more words, so that the entire page read: *For Elly, Who succeeded in changing a suffering man into a loving man. Viktor.*

I was introduced to Viktor Frankl and his work as a graduate student learning to be a counselor. Although I read about logotherapy in my textbooks, their focus was more on Frankl's therapeutic techniques, like paradoxical intention, than on treatment through discovering meaning for one's life. As far as I could tell, paradoxical intention was an ingenious and powerful tool, but at the time, I felt a little cheated; I wanted to know more about how Frankl made use of the human search for meaning in his treatment approaches.

Like many Americans born immediately after World War II, I did not learn about the Holocaust in school. It wasn't until I saw the graphic movie about Auschwitz-Birkenau, *Night and Fog*, while I was in college that I first heard about it. I was devastated and began reading all I could find about the atrocities in an effort to understand how such a thing could happen. My reading continued long past college and graduate school, and it was as part of that reading, rather than my counseling education, that I first read *Man's Search for Meaning*. Viktor Frankl became one of my heroes when, for the first time, I read something hopeful that came out of an individual's direct experience of the Holocaust.

I returned often to *Man's Search for Meaning* for inspiration, and I told parts of Viktor's story to the students I counseled when they shared circumstances that gave them feelings of hopelessness. I hoped Viktor's story might inspire them as it had me. I remember deciding to write his biography for young people on a day when I helped a student into an ambulance. Tommy (not his real name) was a boy who felt there was no future for him in our small New Mexico community, and he was quietly destroying his life by sniffing inhalants. As I walked back into the school on that beautiful spring day, I knew I would start writing this book that summer. Tommy was in eighth grade at the time. He returned to school with a different outlook after a month in treatment. An unexpected result of my research and writing was that I began to use logotherapy more and more in my counseling.

In my research, I have relied heavily on three books, and the majority of the quotations I have used come from them: *Man's Search for Meaning (MSM)*, *Recollections (REC)*, and *When Life Calls Out to Us (WLCO)*. Chapters four and five, the heart of this book, are very much about the experiences Viktor described and analyzed in *MSM*. It isn't necessary for me to go into detail about it here. I will simply say that everyone I've talked to who has read the book has been deeply affected by it. The response has been so positive that I believe *MSM* should be required reading in every American high school.

Recollections is a thin autobiographical volume, very conversational in tone, containing some of Viktor Frankl's earliest memories, anecdotes that flesh out and add new information to the account in *MSM*, and stories of the recreation of his life in Vienna after the Holocaust. It gave me the invaluable sense of Viktor's humanness, his voice, and his broad interests outside of his work. The foreword by one of the book's translators, Joseph Fabry, also offered important insights into Viktor's life and personality.

I am very much indebted to Haddon Klingberg's authorized biography of Viktor and Elly Frankl, *When Life Calls Out to Us (WLCO)*. Klingberg, an American psychologist and professor of psychology, studied under Viktor Frankl and others at the University of Vienna from 1962 to 1963. Klingberg met and recorded interviews with the Frankls over a period of seven years and did additional exhaustive and meticulous research. He provides, first of all, an intimate portrait of Viktor and of his relationship with Elly, including the author's personal reflections. Many of the anecdotes in *WLCO* cannot be found elsewhere, and others expand on or clarify material from other sources. Chapter twelve of *WLCO*, entitled "Controversy, Conflict, and Criticism," was especially helpful in writing the part of chapter seven of this book that describes and seeks to understand some of the less positive responses to Viktor's personality and work.

One other book deserves special mention. I have not quoted from it, but Anita Diamant and Howard Cooper's book, *Living a Jewish Life*, enabled me to check numerous facts about Jewish customs and values.

In December 2002, Elly Frankl graciously allowed me an interview in the home she and Viktor had shared for fifty years on Mariannengasse. She knew nothing more about me than what I had written in a letter to her in November, but, as generous with her time then as she and Viktor had been during his lifetime, she shared with me three full hours that were among the warmest I have spent with someone I didn't know. A former student of Viktor's, Harald Mori, was also present, and the two of them presented me with new insights, anecdotes I had not found in books, and a tour of the apartment and the Frankl archives.

My descriptions of places in Vienna and of Auschwitz-Birkenau come from my visits in 2002 and 1994, respectively, and from information in works listed in the bibliography. The Jüdisches Museum in Vienna helped me get a sense of the overwhelming destruction to the once-thriving Jewish community there, and particularly of the events of Kristallnacht.

SOURCE NOTES BY CHAPTER

Abbreviations for works frequently cited:

MSM: Man's Search for Meaning
REC: Recollections
WLCO: When Life Calls Out to Us

Introduction: Salvation Through Love

The labor detail's forced march: *MSM.*
The visit to St. Stephan's Cathedral: *REC; Vienna: DK Eyewitness Travel Guides.*

Chapter One: A Scholar and a Prankster

Viktor's birth: *REC.*
Description of Viktor's parents and siblings, childhood and teen years: *REC;* "Scientific Lie Detection"; *WLCO.*
Vienna as the birthplace of the Modern Age: *The First Moderns.*
Sigmund Freud and Viktor's correspondence with him: *The First Moderns; Freud: A Life for Our Time; Freud and Beyond; Sigmund Freud: Pioneer of the Mind; REC; WLCO.*
Hitler's early years: *Adolf Hitler; The Life and Death of Adolf Hitler; The Other Victims; The War Against the Jews.*

Chapter Two: Standing on the Shoulders of Giants

Choosing psychiatry: *REC; WLCO.*
Learning from Freud and Adler: *REC; WLCO.*
Early development of logotherapy, youth counseling centers, early work as a psychiatrist: *MSM; REC; WLCO.*

Chapter Three: Hitler Comes to Power

Hitler's takeover of the German government: *Adolf Hitler; The Life and Death of Adolf Hitler;* "Nazi Germany Timeline"; *The Rise and Fall of the Third Reich; The Road to War; The War Against the Jews.*

The Austrian Anschluss and Viktor's and his family's experience of it: *The Austrians; The Devil in Vienna; Hitler's Austria;* exhibits at the Jüdisches Museum; *REC; The Rise and Fall of the Third Reich; This Is Berlin; The War Against the Jews; WLCO.*

Nazi takeover of Czechoslovakia and Poland and establishment of the Final Solution: *The Architect of Genocide; The Life and Death of Adolf Hitler; The Rise and Fall of the Third Reich; The War Against the Jews.*

Euthanasia program: *The Architect of Genocide; REC; The War Against the Jews; WLCO.*

Victor's early romances and his marriage to Tilly Grosser: *REC; WLCO.*

Chapter Four: Say Yes to Life in Spite of Everything

Frankl Family experience at Sperlgymnasium and transport to Theresienstadt: *WLCO.*

Theresienstadt: *I Never Saw Another Butterfly; REC;* "Theresienstadt"; *Theresienstadt; WLCO.*

Auschwitz: *The Architect of Genocide; MSM;* "Mauthausen"; exhibits at the Auschwitz Museum; "Memorial and Museum Auschwitz-Birkenau: The Expansion of the Camp"; *Night and Fog; REC; The War Against the Jews; WLCO.*

Kaufering and Türkheim: *MSM; REC; WLCO.*

Chapter Five: Finding Meaning in Tragedy

Early days after liberation and the writing of *Man's Search for Meaning: MSM; REC;* "St. Stephan's Cathedral"; *The Third Man; WLCO.*

Psychological analysis of the concentration camp experience: *MSM.*

Chapter Six: A Time to Live

Recreating a life with Elly and Gaby in Vienna: author's interview with Elly Frankl and Harald Mori; *MSM; REC; WLCO.*

Chapter Seven: The World Responds

Viktor's work with patients and influence on those who read *Man's Search for Meaning: MSM; REC; Frankl's Choice; WLCO.*

Controversies about Viktor and logotherapy: "Viktor Frankl at Ninety"; *WLCO; The Will to Meaning.*

Logotherapy today: "Debating Human Happiness"; "Viktor Frankl at Ninety"; Viktor Frankl Institut; Viktor Frankl Institute of Logotherapy; *WLCO.*

Chapter Eight: Saying Yes Until the End

Second bar mitzvah: "Adult Bar and Bat Mitzvah"; "Jerusalem"; "The Western Wall"; *WLCO.*

Last years and death: author's interview with Elly Frankl and Harald Mori; *Frankl's Choice; WLCO.*

BIBLIOGRAPHY

BOOKS

Breitman, Richard, *The Architect of Genocide: Himmler and the Final Solution*. New York: Alfred A. Knopf, 1991.

Brook, Stephen, *Vienna: DK Eyewitness Travel Guides*. New York: DK Publishing, Inc., 2002.

Brook-Shepherd, Gordon, *The Austrians: A Thousand-Year Odyssey*. New York: Carroll and Graf Publishers, Inc., 1997.

Bukey, Evan Burr, *Hitler's Austria: Popular Sentiment in the Nazi Era: 1938–1945*. Chapel Hill: University of North Carolina Press, 2000.

Dawidowicz, Lucy S., *The War Against the Jews: 1933–1945*. New York: Bantam Books, 1986.

Diamant, Anita, with Howard Cooper, *Living a Jewish Life: Jewish Traditions, Customs, and Values for Today's Families*. New York: Harper Perennial, 1996.

Everdell, William R., *The First Moderns: Profiles in the Origins of Twentieth-Century Thought*. Chicago: University of Chicago Press, 1997.

Frankl, Viktor Emil, *Bergerlebnis und Sinnerfahrung*. Vienna: Tyrolia-Verlag, 2002.

————, *Man's Search for Meaning*. Trans. Ilse Lasch. Boston: Beacon Press, 1992.

————, *Man's Search for Ultimate Meaning*. New York: Insight Books, 1997.

————, *Recollections: An Autobiography*. Trans. Joseph and Judith Fabry. New York: Perseus Publishing, 2000.

————, *The Will to Meaning: Foundations and Applications of Logotherapy*. New York: New American Library in association with World Publishing Company, 1969.

Friedman, Ina R., *Escape or Die: True Stories of Young People Who Survived the Holocaust*. Reading, Massachusetts: Addison-Wesley Publishing Company, 1982.

————, *The Other Victims: First-Person Stories of Non-Jews Persecuted by the Nazis*. Boston: Houghton Mifflin Company, 1990.

Gay, Peter, *Freud: A Life for Our Time*. New York: W. W. Norton and Company, 1988.

Giblin, James Cross, *The Life and Death of Adolf Hitler*. New York: Clarion Books, 2002.

Greene, Graham, *The Third Man*. New York: Viking Press, 1950.

Klingberg, Haddon, Jr., *When Life Calls Out to Us: The Love and Lifework of Viktor and Elly Frankl*. New York: Doubleday, 2001.

Mitchell, Stephen A. and Margaret J. Black, *Freud and Beyond: A History of Modern Psychoanalytical Thought*. New York: Basic Books, 1995

Orgel, Doris, *The Devil in Vienna*. New York: Dial Press, 1978.

Overy, Richard, and Andrew Wheatcroft, *The Road to War: The Origins of World War II*. New York: Random House, 1989.

Reef, Catherine, *Sigmund Freud: Pioneer of the Mind*. New York: Clarion Books, 2001.

Shirer, William L., *The Rise and Fall of the Third Reich: A History of Nazi Germany*. New York: Simon and Schuster, 1960.

————, *This Is Berlin: Radio Broadcasts from Nazi Germany*. New York: Overlook Press, 1999.

Toland, John, *Adolf Hitler*. Garden City, NY: Anchor Books, 1992.

Troller, Norbert, *Theresienstadt: Hitler's Gift to the Jews*. Trans. Susan E. Cernyak-Spatz. Ed. Joel Shatzky. Chapel Hill: University of North Carolina Press, 1991.

Volavková, Hana, ed., *I Never Saw Another Butterfly: Children's Drawings and Poems from Terezin Concentration Camp, 1942–1944*. Trans. Jeanne Němcovál. New York: Schocken Books, Expanded Second Edition, 1993.

FILMS

Drazen, Ruth Yorkin, *Frankl's Choice*, 2001.

Resnais, Alain, *Night and Fog*, 1955.

WEBSITES

"Children," Holocaust Encyclopedia, www.ushmm.org/wlc/en

"Jerusalem," Microsoft Encarta Online Encyclopedia 2003, www.encarta.msn.com

Jaffe-Gill, Ellen, "Adult Bar and Bat Mitzvah: Meaningful at Every Age,"
United Jewish Communities,
www.ujc.org/content_display.html?ArticleID=1587

"Memorial and Museum Auschwitz-Birkenau: The Expansion of the Camp,"
www.auschwitz-muzeum.oswiecim.pl/html/eng/start/index.php

"Mauthausen," www.remember.org/camps/mauthausen

"Nazi Germany Timeline," www.spartacus.schoolnet.co.uk/GERchron.htm

"Phylacteries, *Mezuzah,* and Torah Scroll,"
www.torah.org/learning/halacha-overview/chapter8.html

"Scientific Lie Detection,"
www.faculty.ncwc.edu/toconnor/315/315lect09b.htm

Scully, Matthew, "Viktor Frankl at Ninety: An Interview,"
www.firstthings.com/ftissues/ft9504/scully.html

Seligman, Martin, "Debating Human Happiness,"
www.slate.com/?id=2072079&entry=2072402

"St. Stephan's Cathedral," www.vienna.cc/english/stephansdom.htm

"Theresienstadt," www.ushmm.org/wlc/article.jsp?ModuleId=10005424

Viktor Frankl Institut, www.logotherapy.univie.ac.at/

Viktor Frankl Institute of Logotherapy, www.logotherapyinstitute.org/

"The Western Wall," www.mosaic.lk.net/g-wall.html

OTHER SOURCES

Auschwitz Museum, Oswiecim, Poland

Elly Frankl and Harald Mori, author interview, December 27, 2002

Jüdisches Museum, Dorotheergasse, Vienna, Austria

For Further Reading

Axelrod, Toby, *Hans and Sophie Scholl: German Resisters of the White Rose*. New York: Rosen Publishing Group, 2001. A biography of the young German brother and sister who gathered with a few friends to resist the Nazis. It details the actions of the entire White Rose group, focusing on Hans and Sophie.

Frankl, Viktor Emil, *Man's Search for Meaning*. Boston: Beacon Press, 1992. Viktor Frankl tells in his own words what it took for him to survive the horrors of four Nazi concentration camps and how the experience impacted his work as a psychiatrist. The second part of the book focuses on the theory and practice of logotherapy and includes anecdotes from the camps and Frankl's psychotherapy practice to illustrate his points.

Friedman, Ina R., *Escape or Die: True Stories of Young People Who Survived the Holocaust*. Reading, Massachusetts: Addison-Wesley Publishing, 1982. A collection of brief first-person accounts of young people's bravery, determination to live, and often luck in escaping the fate Nazis had planned for them. For each country represented, a history of the Jews in that country introduces the stories.

————, *The Other Victims: First-Person Stories of Non-Jews Persecuted by the Nazis*. Boston: Houghton Mifflin Company, 1990. This book shows how widely the Nazis cast their net of destruction to include artists, political dissenters, clergy, homosexuals, Roma, Jehovah's Witnesses, and Slavs. Each personal story is introduced with a clear explanation of the historical context.

Giblin, James Cross, *The Life and Death of Adolf Hitler*. New York: Clarion Books, 2002. This highly readable biography of Hitler gives an objective, historical account of the man, his journey to power, his dictatorship, and his demise while exploring the personal and social events that motivated his actions.

Lobel, Anita, *No Pretty Pictures: A Child of War*. New York: Greenwillow Books, 1998. The beloved children's author and illustrator tells with deep emotion the story of how she and her younger brother survived the Holocaust—first hiding, then being imprisoned, and finally, being liberated. She writes openly and poignantly of how her experiences caused her to hate being Jewish and of how she healed after the war.

Lowry, Lois, *Number the Stars*. New York: Laurel-Leaf Books, 1998. This Newbery Award winner tells the story of a courageous Danish girl who helps save the lives of her Jewish best friend and her friend's family by getting them to neutral Sweden in a fishing boat.

Orgel, Doris, *The Devil in Vienna*. New York: Dial Press, 1978. A novel based on the author's experience as a Jewish child in Vienna. The story centers on the time surrounding the Anschluss and on the seeming betrayal of the main character by her best friend, who joins the Hitler Youth. The book is full of details about Viktor Frankl's city and about how one family escaped.

Reef, Catherine, *Sigmund Freud: Pioneer of the Mind*. New York: Clarion Books, 2001. This biography, written for young people, is a clear, concise introduction to the life and work of the founder of psychoanalysis.

Siegal, Aranka, *Upon the Head of the Goat: A Childhood in Hungary, 1939–1944*. New York: Farrar, Strauss & Giroux, 1981. A warm, personal account of a resourceful Hungarian Jewish family, courageously committed to their own and their community's survival during the five years leading up to their deportation to Auschwitz. A Newbery Honor Book.

Volavková, Hana, ed., *I Never Saw Another Butterfly: Children's Drawings and Poems from Terezin Concentration Camp, 1942–1944*. New York: Schoken Books, 1993 A beautiful collection of color reproductions of the poignant artwork, poems, and journal entries of children and young people imprisoned at Theresienstadt.

Wiesel, Elie, *Dawn*. New York: Bantam Books, 1982. A novel about an eighteen-year-old survivor of Auschwitz and Buchenwald, exploring his moral struggle during one night in Palestine. At dawn he is to execute an English soldier in the fight to establish the state of Israel; as he gets to know the soldier, he asks himself whether his own suffering and the deaths of his friends and family justify what he is about to do.

————, *Night*. New York: Bantam Books, 1982. Elie Wiesel was thirteen years old when he was deported to Auschwitz. This is the story of his survival and his losses. It asks the deep questions about the existence and nature of a God who would allow these horrible experiences, posed by a young boy who was a devout Jew when he entered the camp.

INDEX

Note: Page numbers in *italic* type indicate illustrations.